The Princeton Review

Roadmap to 5th Grade Math: VIRGINIA EDITION

by
Tom
Meltzer

Random House, Inc.
New York

k12.princetonreview.com

This workbook was written by The Princeton Review, one of the nation's leaders in test preparation. The Princeton Review helps millions of students every year prepare for standardized assessments of all kinds. The Princeton Review offers the best way to help students excel on standardized tests.

The Princeton Review is not affiliated with Princeton University or Educational Testing Service.

Princeton Review, L.L.C.
160 Varick Street 12th floor
New York, NY 10013

E-mail: comments@review.com

Published in the United States by Random House, Inc., New York.

ISBN 0-375-75601-9

Editor: Scott Bridi
Development Editor: David Smith
Production Editor: Diahl Ballard
Director of Production: Iam Williams
Design Director: Tina McMaster
Art Director: Neil McMahon
Production Coordinator: Theresa Wiscovitch
Ollie the Ostrich illustrated by Paulo De Freitas Jr.

Manufactured in the United States of America

9 8 7 6 5 4 3 2 1

First Edition

Contents

Acknowledgments

This book, like all Princeton Review books, owes its existence to those who originated and developed The Princeton Review approach to standardized test taking. The insights and strategies of Geoff Martz, Nell Goddin, Paul Foglino, Teresa Chambers, and, of course, Adam Robinson and John Katzman, provided the fertile soil from which this book grew. Thanks also to Scott Bridi for his confidence in my work, which made my job much easier.

Dedication

Dedicated to the Original Carter Family, the great Virginian musicians who wisely advised us all to "keep on the sunny side of life."

Parent/Teacher Introduction

About this Book

The Princeton Review is one of the nation's leaders in test preparation. We prepare more than two million students every year with our courses, books, online services, and software programs. In addition to helping Virginia students with their Standards of Learning (SOL) assessments, we coach students around the country on many other statewide standardized tests, as well as college-entrance exams such as the SAT-I, SAT-II, PSAT, and ACT. Our strategies and techniques are unique and, most important, successful. Our goal is to reinforce skills that students have been taught in the classroom and to show them how to apply those skills to the specific format and structure of the Virginia SOL mathematics test for grade 5.

Roadmap to 5th Grade Math: Virginia Edition contains three basic elements: lessons, test-preparation practice, and practice tests. Each lesson (or "mile") focuses on a specific skill such as multiplication or decimals. Each mile includes a fun, interactive activity that reinforces the skill that is introduced. Each activity is followed by focused test preparation that encourages students to refine the skill they practiced in the activity. An answer key for the miles begins on page 141.

The book also contains two full-length practice tests. The practice tests will help you assess which skills students should review and improve upon before they take the SOL mathematics test. Before students begin taking the practice tests, review page 104 with them. This page contains detailed instructions for taking the practice tests as if they were the actual Virginia SOL test. Explanations for the correct answers to the questions on both practice tests are available beginning on page 165.

We've also provided a Progress Chart as a way to encourage and motivate students. The Progress Chart is broken up into forty-five miles, or lessons, to help students see how far they've come in their preparation. Studying for any test can be difficult for young students, and it is as important to encourage good study habits as it is to remediate students' weaknesses. Be vigilant about reminding students how well they are doing and how much they've learned. Building confidence can significantly improve students' scores on any standardized test.

Before students begin their test preparation, take a moment to review the table of contents and to flip through the lessons in the book. We've tried to present the material in such a way that each skill presented builds on the previous one, but we realize that every student and every class have different strengths and weaknesses. There will be no harm done if students work on the lessons out of sequence.

About the Virginia Standards of Learning Mathematics Test

Fifth-grade students in Virginia will be required to take the Virginia Standards of Learning (SOL) test in mathematics. The test contains sixty multiple-choice questions. Students must choose one of four answer choices for each question. For each answer choice they select, they must fill in the corresponding bubble on an answer sheet. The test is *untimed*, so they should not get anxious about finishing as quickly as possible.

Ten of the sixty multiple-choice questions will be field-test items that do not count toward students' test scores. Because there is no way to differentiate the field-test items from the scored items, students should answer all of the questions as if they count toward their scores. Students' test scores are reported as failing, proficient, or advanced. Students' SOL test scores may be used as a factor in determining grade promotion or retention. The two levels of passing test scores, as of 2002, are explained below.

Proficient: The student answers at least 68% (34 out of 50) of the scored items correctly.

Advanced: The student answers at least 92% (46 out of 50) of the scored items correctly.

Students' test scores are reported as whole scores and in terms of five separate reporting categories. The categories, or content areas, for the fifth-grade Virginia SOL mathematics assessment are Number and Number Sense, Computation and Estimation, Measurement and Geometry, Probability and Statistics, and Patterns, Functions, and Algebra. Test results are reported in terms of these categories so teachers can easily identify those content areas for which students may require more instruction.

> **Note:** Check with the Virginia Department of Education for the most recent information about test-score reporting. Also, check with your school district for the test-administration date in your area.

Check the Virginia Department of Education Web site for updates about the Virginia standards of learning at www.pen.k12.va.us/VDOE/Instruction/sol.html.

The fifth-grade mathematics test blueprints, which include the standards assessed on the test, can be found at www.pen.k12.va.us/VDOE/Assessment/soltests/math5.html.

Practical Notes for the Testing Day

- Students will not be penalized for choosing wrong answers. There is no "guessing penalty," so students should answer every question on the test.
- Students will be allowed to use scratch paper during the test.
- Students will be allowed to use standard and metric rulers during the test.
- Students will be allowed to use a protractor during the test.
- The test is administered in two sections. Students will be allowed to use a four-function calculator during one of the two sections. However, calculator use for the section that contains Computation and Estimation questions is prohibited.

Student Introduction

Student Introduction

About This Book

We're guessing that you don't like taking tests. Given the choice, you'd never take another test again, right? Well, *Roadmap to 5th Grade Math* makes it fun to learn how to take tests. The book includes games to play, puzzles to finish, and riddles to answer.

Every lesson in this book is another "mile" on a trip that ends with you doing your best on the Virginia Standards of Learning (SOL) mathematics test. Each mile reviews a skill that you'll be tested on when you take the SOL test. We'll take you step-by-step through all the basics. Check your work in the miles by looking at the answer key that begins on page 141. And after you review, you will get a chance to show what you know. What could be more fun than that? Track how far you have come on the Progress Chart on pages 6 and 7 by marking every mile after you've finished it.

You'll be an expert at math in no time at all. The only thing left to do will be for you to show your parents and teachers what you've learned by acing your SOL math test. And just in case you're worried about how well you'll do, we've given you two complete practice tests to take after you finish all the miles. These practice tests can show you exactly how great your math skills are! Beginning on page 165, we provide answers and detailed explanations for all of the questions on both practice tests.

You still might not like tests. That's okay. By the time you get to the end of *Roadmap to 5th Grade Math: Virginia Edition*, you'll be ready to do your best on them!

What Else Can I Do?

There are other things you can do to prepare for the Virginia SOL mathematics test.

- **Ask questions.** If you are confused after you finish a mile (or even just one question), ask a parent or teacher for help. Asking questions is the best way to make sure that you understand how to do your best!
- **Read.** Read everything you can. Read the newspaper, magazines, books, plays, poems, comics, and even the back of your cereal box. The more you read, the better you will be able to read. And the better you read, the more likely you are to do well on the SOL math test. Many of the questions on the math test will be word problems. If you can't read and understand the problems, you won't have a chance to show all the math you know.
- **Practice.** Every time you go to the grocery store, make dinner, play baseball, or count sheep at night, math is around you. Use real-life opportunities to practice the math you know. Add the prices of the groceries in your cart while you're waiting in line at the store. See if your sum matches what comes up on the cash register. Keep track of how many hits you got on your little league team. Turn that into a fraction of your total at-bats. Every day there's more math to do, and the great thing is that it's almost the same math that's on your SOL test!
- **Eat well and get a good night's sleep.** Your body doesn't work well when you don't eat good food and get enough sleep. Neither does your brain. On the night before the test, make sure you go to bed at your normal time. You should also eat a healthy breakfast on the testing day. You will do better if you are awake and alert while taking the SOL mathematics test.

This is just the beginning of the road. There are great things to learn ahead. So buckle your seatbelt and get ready to travel the first mile to math excellence!

Directions: Cross off or color in each mile marker as you complete each activity.

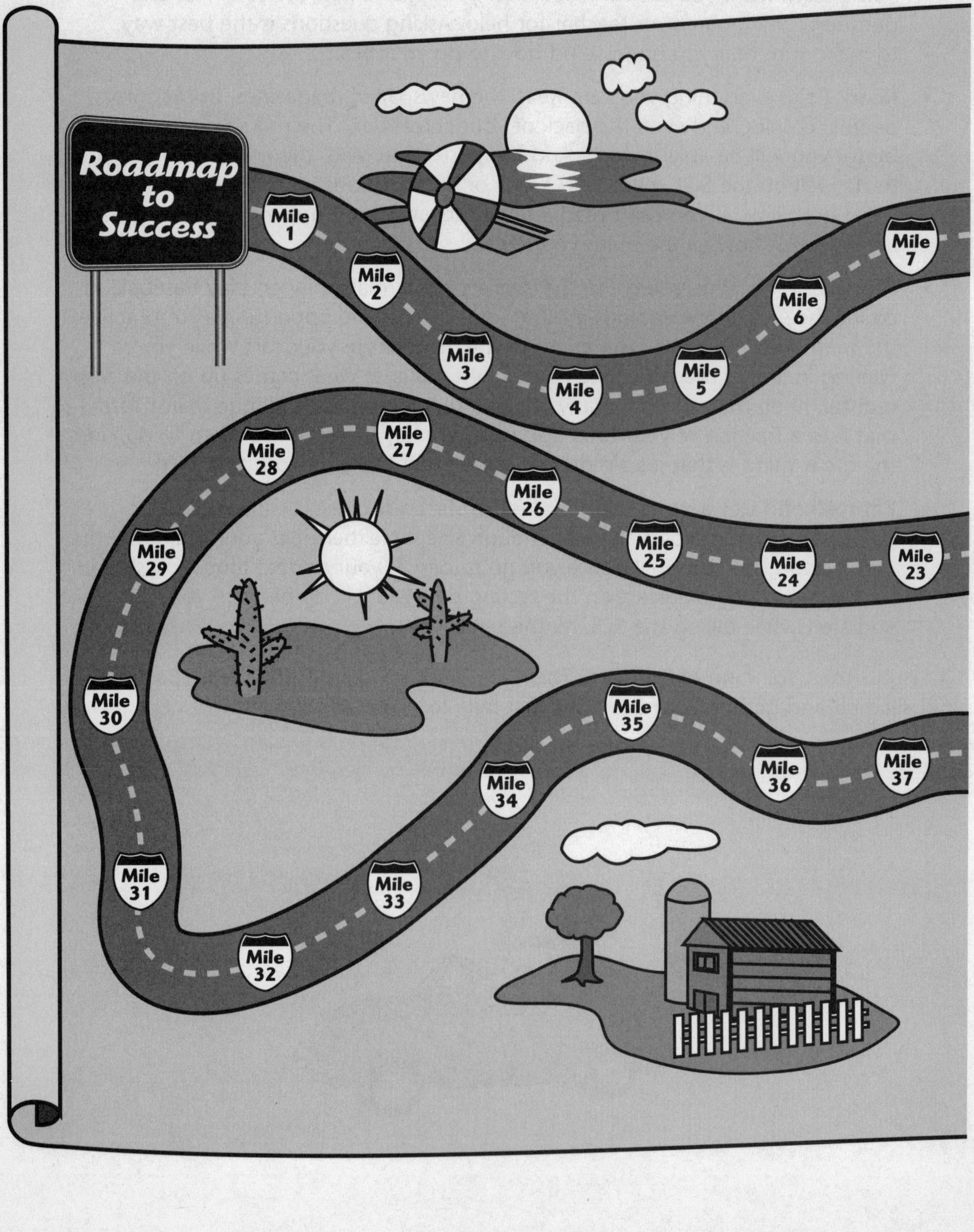

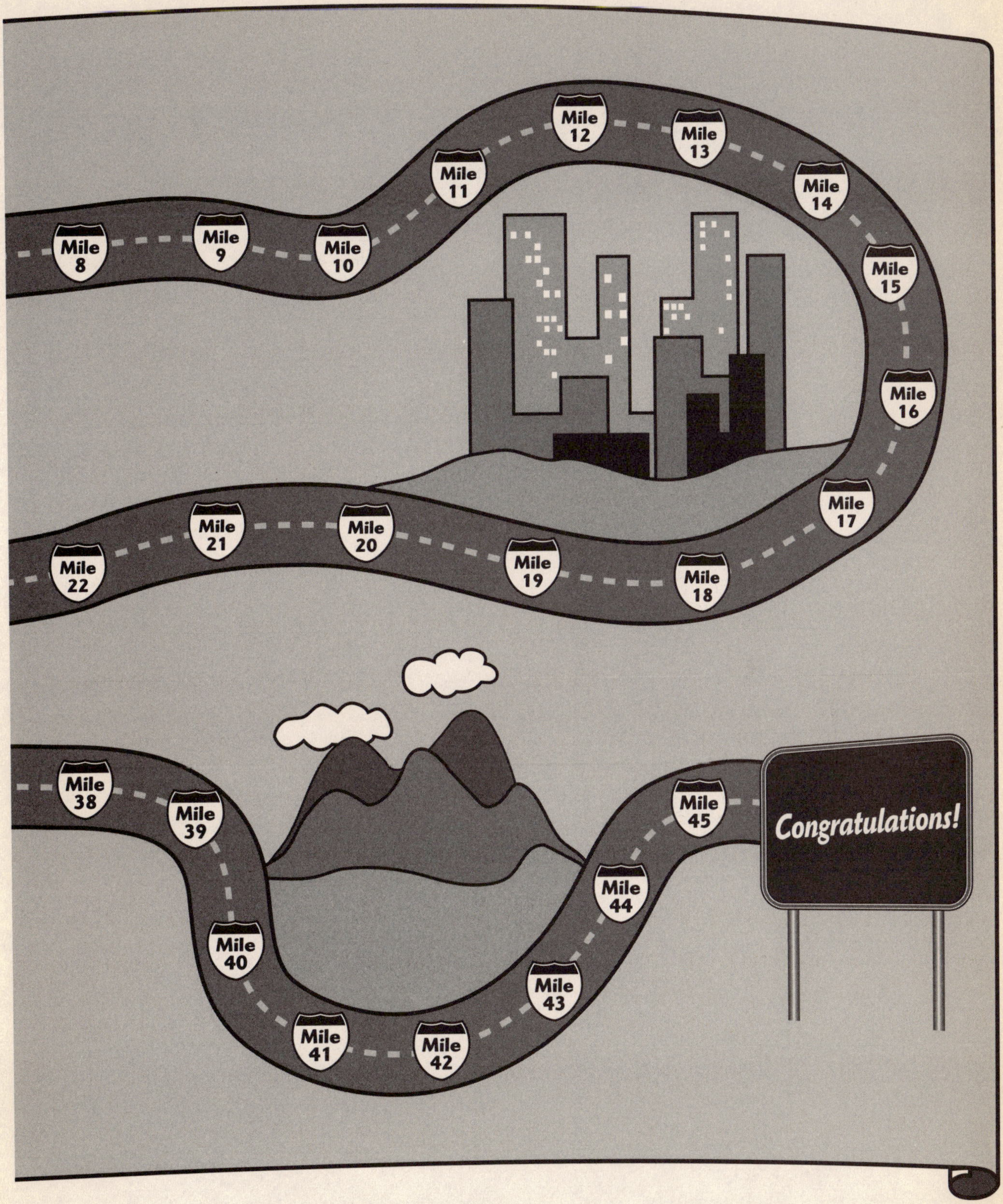
Mile 8
Mile 9
Mile 10
Mile 11
Mile 12
Mile 13
Mile 14
Mile 15
Mile 16
Mile 17
Mile 18
Mile 19
Mile 20
Mile 21
Mile 22
Mile 38
Mile 39
Mile 40
Mile 41
Mile 42
Mile 43
Mile 44
Mile 45
Congratulations!

Mile by Mile

Before You Begin: Process of Elimination (POE)

On the Virginia grade five math SOL test, each multiple-choice question has four answer choices. You have to pick an answer choice for each question.

What if you don't know the right answer? Don't worry about it. You still might be able to pick the right answer if you use **Process of Elimination (POE).** To use POE, you have to look for choices that you *know* are wrong. Then eliminate, or cross out, those choices.

Imagine that you are a contestant on a game show. The host asks you the question: "What is the capital of China?" If you answer correctly, you will win one million dollars! You are given four choices.

○ **A** Richmond

○ **B** London

○ **C** New York

○ **D** Beijing

Do you know the capital of China? Even if you don't, you can still win the money. You can use POE to get rid of the answer choices that you know are wrong. Then choose from the choices that are left.

Let's see how this works. Look at the four answer choices again. You probably know some of them. Which cities are definitely not the capital of China? You know that Richmond is the capital of Virginia. Richmond is not in China at all, so you can eliminate **A.** London is in England, not China, so you can eliminate **B**. You know that New York is in the United States, not in China, so you can eliminate **C**, too. That leaves you with **D**, *Beijing*. Beijing must be the capital of China. Even if you didn't know the capital of China, using Process of Elimination made you a millionaire!

But what if you can't eliminate all of the wrong answer choices? That's okay. You still have a better chance of picking the correct answer. You always start with four answer choices on the math SOL test. If you have no idea how to answer a question, you don't have a good chance of picking the correct answer choice. If you eliminate one or two answer choices, you have a better chance of picking the correct one. This can be a boost to your score on any test you take.

Take a look at this example of how POE can help you with a multiple-choice math question. This question may seem difficult without using POE first.

▶ **Tiffany took 51 pictures of her class trip to the zoo. She wants to give all the pictures to her 3 friends. If she gives each friend the same number of pictures, how many pictures does each friend get?**

○ **A** 4

○ **B** 8

○ **C** 17

○ **D** 25

Let's use Process of Elimination before you choose the correct answer.

Look at **A.** If each friend gets 4 pictures, Tiffany will only give away 12 pictures. Because she has 51 pictures to give away, you can eliminate **A.**

Look at **B.** It's possible that each friend would get 8 pictures, but will Tiffany have any left over? If you round up 8 to 10, you can estimate that she gave away about 30 pictures. Eliminate **B** because she has 51 pictures to give away.

Look at **C.** Tiffany may have enough pictures to give 17 of them to each of her friends. Let's say she gave her friend Carley 17 pictures. Then Tiffany would have 34 pictures left to give to her other 2 friends ($51 - 17 = 34$). It seems like she'll have enough pictures to give 17 to each of the 3 friends. This seems like a good answer, so keep it, but don't fill in an answer bubble until you've seen all the choices.

Look at **D.** Tiffany does not have enough pictures to give 25 of them to each of her 3 friends. Let's say her friend Jimmy got 25 pictures. Then Tiffany would only have 26 pictures left to give to her other 2 friends. She definitely won't be able to give 25 pictures to each of her 3 friends. Eliminate **D.**

That leaves you with **C.** Tiffany has enough pictures to give 17 to each of her 3 friends. You can check your answer by adding $17 + 17 + 17$. This adds up to 51. **C** is the correct answer. And using Process of Elimination helped you find it!

OK, we'll be honest. You probably won't be able to eliminate all three of the incorrect answers that come with each question on the Virginia SOL test. But you get the idea. Process of Elimination can be very helpful when you get stuck on a question, even if you can only eliminate one or two answer choices.

MILE 1: COMPARING NUMBERS

Directions: Read statements 1 through 5 and follow the directions for each one. Then look at the shape you drew for each statement. Use the code breaker at the bottom of the page to find a letter that goes with each shape you drew. Write that letter in the space provided next to the question. When you are finished, the letters will spell out the name of a famous rock star. Who is it?

________	1.	If the first number has a greater value, circle it. If the second number has a greater value, draw a square around it.	**7,405,634 and 7,398,113**
________	2.	Draw a square around the first number if it is greater than the second number. Circle the second number if it is greater than the first number.	**1,134,509 and 1,132,798**
________	3.	Two of the three numbers are equal. If the first number is different from the other two, circle it. If the second number is the different one, draw a star around it. If the third number is the different one, draw a diamond around it.	**4,560,001 and 4,506,001 and four million five hundred sixty thousand and one**
________	4.	Which number is greater? If the first number is greater, draw an "X" through it. If the second number is greater, draw a diamond around it.	**5,468,376 and 5,498,102**
________	5.	Which number is greater? If the first number is greater, circle it. If the second number is greater, draw an "X" through it.	**7,235,002 and seven million, two hundred fifty three thousand and two**

Secret Code Breaker

☆	×	○	□	◇
V	**S**	**E**	**L**	**I**

► The famous rock star is ______________________________.

Directions: Read each question carefully. Fill in the bubble next to your answer choice for each question.

1 Which statement is correct?

- ○ A 1,350,277 > 1,402,755
- ○ B 1,565,071 > 1,480,036
- ○ C 1,800,005 > 1,810,001
- ○ D 1,006,388 > 1,256,799

2 Which statement is true?

- ○ F 7,902,538 < 7,885,466
- ○ G 7,265,388 < 7,250,145
- ○ H 7,185,664 < 7,190,912
- ○ J 7,461,569 < 7,317,933

3 Which is correct?

- ○ A 5,545,912 > 5,481,702
- ○ B 5,391,207 > 5,438,225
- ○ C 5,820,681 > 5,926,434
- ○ D 5,700,402 > 5,708,401

4 Which is true?

- ○ F 3,302,673 < 3,299,781
- ○ G 3,782,576 < 3,790,413
- ○ H 3,550,281 < 3,421,738
- ○ J 355,712 < 3,451,713

5 Which statement is correct?

- ○ A 6,166,920 < 6,163,347
- ○ B 6,714,699 < 6,702,820
- ○ C 6,455,791 < 6,408,777
- ○ D 6,810,501 < 6,915,724

When you take the Virginia SOL math test, it is important for you to know the difference between the "greater than" (>) and "less than" (<) symbols. If you realize that the symbol is always supposed to point to the smaller number, you should have no trouble remembering which is which. For example, 80 < 100 means that 80 is less than 100. (Notice how the symbol points in the direction of 80, which is the smaller number.) 53 > 47 means that 53 is greater than 47. (Notice how the symbol points to 47, the smaller number.)

MILE 2: PLACE VALUE

You already know that 200 is bigger than 20. Why? Because in 200 the 2 is in the hundreds place, which means that the 2 stands for two hundreds. In 20 the 2 is in the tens place, which means that the 2 stands for two tens. (If you add 100 and 100, you get 200.)

A number with nine digits, such as 123,456,789, has nine place values. From left to right, the **place values** are hundred millions, ten millions, millions, hundred thousands, ten thousands, thousands, hundreds, tens, and ones.

Directions: Match the numbers with their correct written forms. The letters will spell the last name of the twentieth U.S. president—and also a popular cartoon character. Here's a hint: Think about the place values of the numbers to help you complete this matching.

1. _____	one thousand one hundred fifteen	R)	99,012,001
2. _____	two hundred seventy million, nine hundred eighty-nine thousand, one hundred twelve	E)	2,000,710
3. _____	ninety-nine million, twelve thousand, one	I)	375,525,615
4. _____	seven hundred nineteen thousand, three hundred sixty-five	L)	7,933,222
5. _____	three hundred seventy-five million, five hundred twenty-five thousand, six hundred fifteen	F)	719,365
6. _____	two million, seven hundred ten	A)	270,989,112
7. _____	seven million, nine hundred thirty-three thousand, two hundred twenty-two	D)	12,916
8. _____	twelve thousand, nine hundred sixteen	G)	1,115

▶ The last name of the twentieth president and a popular cartoon character is

_______________________________.

Directions: Read each question carefully. Fill in the bubble next to your answer choice for each question.

1 As Karen rides in a car with her parents, she passes a sign that says that Lookout Mountain is 12,516 feet high. What digit is in the tens place?

- ○ A 1
- ○ B 2
- ○ C 5
- ○ D 6

2 The population of Norfolk is 234,400. The population of Richmond is 197,790. What place value has the same digit for both cities?

- ○ F Ten thousands
- ○ G One thousands
- ○ H Hundreds
- ○ J Ones

3 Consider the number 342,059,218. What digit is in the hundred thousands place?

- ○ A 0
- ○ B 2
- ○ C 3
- ○ D 5

4 How do you write two hundred thirty-five thousand, six hundred ninety-eight in standard form?

- ○ F 23,506,098
- ○ G 2,350,698
- ○ H 235,698
- ○ J 200,035,698

5 In the number 23,056, how many hundreds are there?

- ○ A Five
- ○ B Three
- ○ C Two
- ○ D Zero

Remember that zeros are very important. By itself a zero equals nothing, but in numbers a zero holds a place value.

MILE 3: ROUNDING NUMBERS

You can **round numbers** to make them easier to deal with. You can round *up* or *down* to the nearest ten, hundred, thousand, and so on. If you want to round to the nearest hundred, you should look at the digit in the tens place. If that digit is less than 5, you should round the hundreds down. If that digit is 5 or greater, you should round the hundreds up.

So if you are rounding the number 372 to the nearest hundred, you would look at the digit in the tens place (7). Because 7 is greater than 5, you would round up to 400.

Directions: The following chart tells you how far each of the planets is from the Sun. Round each number of miles to the nearest hundred thousand.

Distance from the Sun in Miles		
Mercury	35,991,000 ⟶	
Venus	67,246,000 ⟶	
Earth	92,956,000 ⟶	
Mars	141,665,000 ⟶	
Jupiter	483,732,000 ⟶	
Saturn	886,843,000 ⟶	
Uranus	1,784,320,000 ⟶	
Neptune	2,794,929,000 ⟶	
Pluto	3,675,253,000 ⟶	

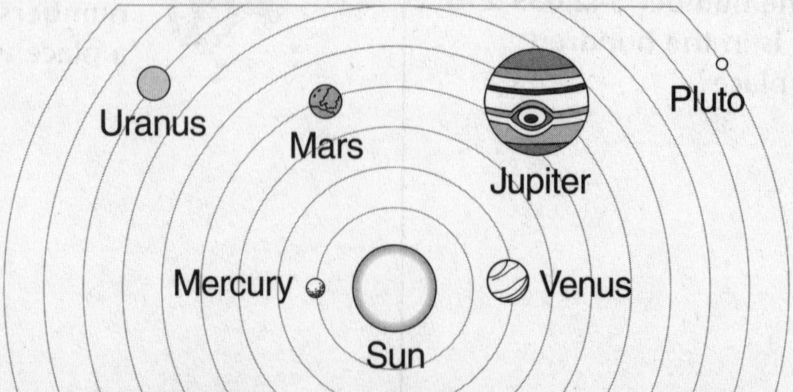

Directions: Read each question carefully. Fill in the bubble next to your answer choice for each question.

1 The value of 5,190,716 rounded to the nearest hundred thousand is —

- ○ A 5,200,000
- ○ B 5,190,000
- ○ C 5,100,000
- ○ D 5,000,000

2 The value of 3,729,038 rounded to the nearest ten thousand is —

- ○ F 3,700,000
- ○ G 3,710,000
- ○ H 3,720,000
- ○ J 3,730,000

3 The value of 8,451,271 rounded to the nearest hundred thousand is —

- ○ A eight million
- ○ B eight million, five hundred thousand
- ○ C eight million, four hundred thousand
- ○ D eight million, four hundred fifty thousand

4 What is the value of 3,059,602 rounded to the nearest thousand?

- ○ F 3,100,000
- ○ G 3,060,000
- ○ H 3,059,000
- ○ J 3,059,500

5 The value of 5,682,418 rounded to the nearest million is —

- ○ A 6,000,000
- ○ B 5,000,000
- ○ C 5,700,000
- ○ D 5,600,000

If the place that's being rounded has a "9" in it, and it's being rounded up, you should do two things. First, change the "9" to a "0." Second, add one to the value of the digit to the left of the place that's being rounded. For example, if you round 129,743 to the nearest thousand, the "9" would be rounded up because there is a "7" in the hundreds place. In this case, you'd follow the two steps above. If you change the "9" to a "0" and add 1 to the digit to the left (2), you'd see that 129,743 rounded to the nearest thousand is 130,000.

Mile 4: Addition and Subtraction

When you add two or more numbers, the result is called a **sum.** When you subtract two numbers, the result is called a **difference.** Addition and subtraction problems can be written horizontally

$$5 + 8 = 13 \qquad 20 - 16 = 4$$

or vertically

$$\begin{array}{r} 5 \\ +\ 8 \\ \hline \end{array} \qquad \begin{array}{r} 20 \\ -\ 16 \\ \hline \end{array}$$

Directions: Find the sums and differences in the following problems in order to complete the cross-number puzzle.

Across

1. 238 + 227 =
3. 9,030 − 1,189 =
5. 198 + 56 =
7. 5095 + 2995 =
8. 1,134 − 356 =

Down

1. 1,700 + 2,578 =
2. 556 − 22 =
4. 117 + 48 =
5. 4,242 − 1,454 =
6. 858 − 359 =

Directions: Read each question carefully. Fill in the bubble next to your answer choice for each question.

1 2,475 + 651 =

- ○ A 3,024
- ○ B 3,026
- ○ C 3,126
- ○ D 3,136

2 778 − 89 =

- ○ F 511
- ○ G 589
- ○ H 680
- ○ J 689

3 8,004 + 4,598 =

- ○ A 12,592
- ○ B 12,602
- ○ C 12,692
- ○ D 12,798

4 7,129 − 2,577 =

- ○ F 4,552
- ○ G 4,696
- ○ H 5,429
- ○ J 5,542

5 7,801 − 87 =

- ○ A 899
- ○ B 6,931
- ○ C 7,704
- ○ D 7,714

Be careful when you carry numbers, or regroup, in addition or subtraction. If you forget to carry numbers, you will come up with an incorrect answer. Sometimes that incorrect answer will be among the answer choices. If you carry numbers carefully, you will avoid making careless mistakes.

MILE 5: MULTIPLICATION

When you multiply two or more numbers, the answer is called the **product.** The numbers you multiply are called **factors.**

Example 1: $98 \times 36 = 3{,}528$

Example 2:

$$\begin{array}{r} 238 \\ \times\ 56 \\ \hline 13{,}328 \end{array}$$

Directions: Multiply these numbers. Then use the code box at the bottom of the page to find a corresponding letter for each product. The letters should be placed in the same order as the multiplication problems below. After you put all of the letters in order, you will spell out the name of a famous mathematician.

1. $\begin{array}{r} 18 \\ \times 9 \\ \hline \end{array}$

2. $\begin{array}{r} 92 \\ \times 35 \\ \hline \end{array}$

3. $\begin{array}{r} 237 \\ \times 83 \\ \hline \end{array}$

4. $\begin{array}{r} 175 \\ \times 25 \\ \hline \end{array}$

5. $\begin{array}{r} 77 \\ \times 9 \\ \hline \end{array}$

6. $\begin{array}{r} 692 \\ \times 76 \\ \hline \end{array}$

7. $\begin{array}{r} 437 \\ \times 24 \\ \hline \end{array}$

8. $\begin{array}{r} 47 \\ \times 3 \\ \hline \end{array}$

9. $\begin{array}{r} 293 \\ \times 122 \\ \hline \end{array}$

10. $\begin{array}{r} 85 \\ \times 17 \\ \hline \end{array}$

11. $\begin{array}{r} 719 \\ \times 329 \\ \hline \end{array}$

N 52,592	T 35,746	I 162	A 19,671	O 1,445	N 236,551
E 10,488	A 4,375	S 3,220	C 693	W 141	

► What is the name of the famous mathematician?

____

Directions: Read each question carefully. Fill in the bubble next to your answer choice for each question.

1 $\begin{array}{r} 29 \\ \times\ 14 \\ \hline \end{array}$

- ○ A 126
- ○ B 335
- ○ C 406
- ○ D 528

2 If you multiply 35 and 56, what is the product?

- ○ F 1,960
- ○ G 1,500
- ○ H 1,492
- ○ J 1,356

3 $\begin{array}{r} 124 \\ \times\ 78 \\ \hline \end{array}$

- ○ A 8,672
- ○ B 9,342
- ○ C 9,642
- ○ D 9,672

4 What is 61 × 249?

- ○ F 17,249
- ○ G 16,289
- ○ H 16,189
- ○ J 15,189

5 $\begin{array}{r} 472 \\ \times\ 37 \\ \hline \end{array}$

- ○ A 17,464
- ○ B 19,304
- ○ C 19,864
- ○ D 170,684

6 What is the product of 36 and 84?

- ○ F 2,604
- ○ G 3,024
- ○ H 3,446
- ○ J 4,711

Division is the reverse of multiplication. You can use division to check your answers to multiplication problems. If your answer is correct, you can divide your product by one of the numbers you multiplied and get the other number you multiplied.

Mile 6: Division

When you divide two numbers, the answer is called the **quotient.** If you divide 43 by 4, the quotient is 10 R3, or 10 with a remainder of 3. The **remainder** is the number left over after you find the quotient. The number to be divided is called the **dividend** (in this case it's 43). The **divisor** is the number you are dividing into the dividend (in this case it's 4).

Directions: Find the quotients and remainders for each of the division problems below. When you are finished, list the remainders for all of the problems from least to greatest on a separate sheet of paper. Then write the letters from the problems next to the matching remainders you wrote in your list. When you read the letters in this order, you will find the name of a popular singer!

1. T $12\overline{)375}$

2. N $5\overline{)539}$

3. I $7\overline{)86}$

4. B $11\overline{)748}$

5. R $6\overline{)385}$

6. S $8\overline{)71}$

7. Y $9\overline{)627}$

8. A $11\overline{)208}$

9. R $12\overline{)155}$

10. E $7\overline{)299}$

11. S $15\overline{)7,543}$

12. P $15\overline{)98}$

13. E $10\overline{)139}$

► Who is the popular singer?

____

Directions: Read each question carefully. Fill in the bubble next to your answer choice for each question.

1 Jo's father baked cupcakes for Jo's birthday party. He baked 18 cupcakes and then put them in boxes. Each box held 4 cupcakes. How many cupcakes were in the unfilled box?

- ○ A 4
- ○ B 3
- ○ C 2
- ○ D 1

2 Bob made $80 last week raking leaves for his neighbors. He worked 5 days to earn this amount. If he earned the same amount each day, how much money did he make each day?

- ○ F $14
- ○ G $16
- ○ H $20
- ○ J $22

3 $4\overline{)256}$ =

- ○ A 68
- ○ B 64
- ○ C 45
- ○ D 32

4 8 R4 is a solution to which of the following problems?

- ○ F $4\overline{)84}$
- ○ G $6\overline{)72}$
- ○ H $8\overline{)68}$
- ○ J $8\overline{)48}$

5 1,710 ÷ 7 =

- ○ A 244 R1
- ○ B 244 R2
- ○ C 244 R5
- ○ D 245 R2

Division seems more complicated than multiplication, but you can always check your work by multiplying the divisor by the quotient and then adding in the remainder. The number you get should be the same as the dividend. Check out the problem below for an example of how this would work.

$$\begin{array}{r} 4 \text{ R4} \\ 24\overline{)100} \end{array}$$

In this problem, 24 is the divisor, 4 is the quotient, 4 is the remainder, and 100 is the dividend. To check the answer, multiply 24 by 4 and add 4. 24 × 4 = 96, and 96 + 4 = 100, which is the dividend. So you know that the answer is correct!

Mile 7: Word Problems

Directions: Read the story and solve the problems as you read them.

The fifth-grade French club decided to have a bake sale to raise money for club activities. Kathy, the club president, was chosen to organize the sale. She asked if anyone wanted to volunteer to bake something.

Doug said that he would bake 3 cakes. Patty and Amy each agreed to bake 1 dozen peanut butter cookies. Karl said he could bake $1\frac{1}{2}$ dozen chocolate chip cookies.

1. *How many individual cookies will be baked?* __________

"Anybody else?" asked a very pleased Kathy. Everybody seemed so excited by the sale.

Ms. Lunnette, their French teacher, spoke up. "I can bake a chocolate torte, which is a French cake. We can also sell cups of milk and coffee to go with the sweets." Everyone thought that was a great idea.

On the day of the bake sale, everyone brought their goodies and the prices were set. Patty and Amy sold their cookies for $0.25 each. Karl's cookies were extra big so he sold them for $0.40 each. Doug sold his angel food cake for $1.25 per slice, his devil's food cake for $1.50 per slice, and his carrot cake for $1.00 per slice. Ms. Lunette's torte was $1.75 per slice. Coffee and milk were 50 cents per cup.

2. *How many slices of devil's food cake can someone buy for $4.50?* __________
3. *If the angel food cake is cut into 8 slices, how much money could Doug raise by selling the whole cake?* __________

Mr. Alvarez, the English teacher, bought 2 cookies from Patty and 1 from Karl. He also bought a cup of coffee.

4. *How much did Mr. Alvarez spend?* __________

Jimmy looked hungrily at Ms. Lunnette's chocolate torte. "I'd sure like to have a piece of that, Ms. Lunnette, but I don't have enough money." So Jimmy bought a slice of Doug's carrot cake and a cup of milk.

5. *How much money did Jimmy spend?* __________

At the end of the day, almost everything was sold. The French club had raised a lot of money for its activities.

Directions: Read each question carefully. Fill in the bubble next to your answer choice for each question.

1 Enrique loves to bake. He baked 30 chocolate chip cookies one day and gave $\frac{1}{2}$ of them to his friend Paula. Of the remaining cookies, his family ate $\frac{1}{3}$ of them. How many cookies are left?

- ○ A 20
- ○ B 15
- ○ C 10
- ○ D 8

2 Aiko went hiking through the woods at a nearby state park. She knows the importance of keeping a steady pace. She hiked at a rate of $2\frac{1}{2}$ miles per hour. What is the distance she hiked in 3 hours?

- ○ F $9\frac{1}{2}$ miles
- ○ G $7\frac{1}{2}$ miles
- ○ H $5\frac{1}{2}$ miles
- ○ J $4\frac{1}{2}$ miles

3 Martha and her family drove 450 miles from their vacation in Florida to their home in Charlotte. It took them 9 hours to drive this distance. On average, how far did the family travel in one hour?

- ○ A 60 miles
- ○ B 50 miles
- ○ C 40 miles
- ○ D 35 miles

4 Marco performed a strange experiment. He wanted to figure out how many feet he could walk in one minute. After timing himself, he found that he can walk 360 feet per minute! Based on this rate, how many feet does he walk per second?

- ○ F 60
- ○ G 30
- ○ H 15
- ○ J 6

For some problems you can check your answers by making an estimate based on the numbers given to you. Estimate by rounding numbers up or down. This will help you figure out if the answer choice you picked is correct.

Mile 8: Estimating

When you **estimate**, you find a number that is close to the exact amount or number. So instead of multiplying 28 × 11 to get the exact answer, you can estimate if you round 28 up to 30 and 11 down to 10. If you multiply 30 × 10, your estimate should be 300. The exact answer is 308. 300 is a good estimate because it's close to the exact answer.

Directions: Rewrite each problem with rounded numbers first and then multiply or divide the rounded numbers. Find the estimates in the code box at the bottom of the page and then cross out those boxes. Then arrange the letters of the remaining boxes according to their numbers from *greatest* to *least*. You will spell out the answer to the question at the bottom of the page.

1. 33 × 8 × ____ Estimate:	2. 87 × 12 × ____ Estimate:	3. 48 × 54 × ____ Estimate:	4. 137 × 73 × ____ Estimate:	5. 243 × 22 × ____ Estimate:
6. 9)44)‾‾‾ Estimate:	7. 11)87)‾‾‾ Estimate:	8. 18)119)‾‾‾ Estimate:	9. 59)181)‾‾‾ Estimate:	10. 67)142)‾‾‾ Estimate:

O 550	**O** 110	**N** 3	**I** 380	**T** 4	**B** 9	**H** 2,500	**C** 89	**R** 900	**L** 240
K 50	**U** 300	**G** 700	**I** 6	**J** 4,800	**D** 420	**V** 9,800	**S** 10	**M** 2	**L** 490

► I don't like my cereal too hot, nor do I like it too cold. I like to wander around the forest and enter houses when no one is home. Who am I?

Directions: Read each question carefully. Fill in the bubble next to your answer choice for each question.

1 Janet was on vacation in Maine with her family. Each day she kept a record of how many miles her family drove.

Day	Miles
Monday	112
Tuesday	68
Wednesday	124

On average, what is the *best* estimate of the number of miles Janet and her family traveled per day for the three days listed above?

- ○ **A** 140 miles
- ○ **B** 120 miles
- ○ **C** 100 miles
- ○ **D** 70 miles

2 Which is the *best* estimate of 54,815 – 8,943?

- ○ **F** A little more than 7,000
- ○ **G** Between 20,000 and 25,000
- ○ **H** A little less than 40,000
- ○ **J** A little more than 45,000

3 If you estimate 76 × 42, which of the following is closest to the actual product?

- ○ **A** 280
- ○ **B** 320
- ○ **C** 2,800
- ○ **D** 3,200

4 Carlos's school was having a bake sale to raise money to build a stage for the school play. Carlos spent 4 days baking 117 cookies for the bake sale.

What is the closest estimate of the average number of cookies he baked per day?

- ○ **F** 30
- ○ **G** 25
- ○ **H** 20
- ○ **J** 15

You can estimate by rounding numbers. When you round numbers, always remember to round up if the digit on the right is 5 or more. You should round down if the digit on the right is less than 5.

Mile 9: Decimals

Decimals are numbers that have a decimal point and one or more numbers to the right of the decimal point. Each place in a decimal has a name.

Example:

1.7238 →	1	.	7	2	3	8
	ones		tenths	hundredths	thousandths	ten-thousandths

1.7238 is the same as the fraction $1\frac{7,238}{10,000}$.

A decimal model can be used to represent a decimal. Here is the decimal model for the number 1.14, or one and fourteen hundredths.

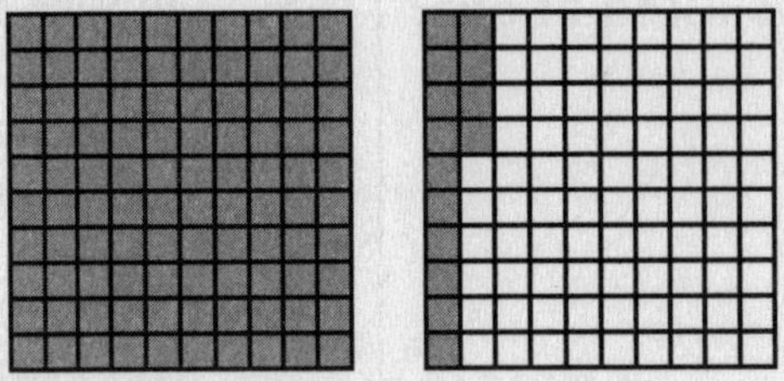

Directions: Match the decimal on the left with the words that state the name of the decimal on the right. The letters will spell out the last name of a popular television family.

1. ______	4.05	O)	four and fifty-five one-hundredths
2. ______	4.5005	S)	four and five one-hundredths
3. ______	4.055	P)	four and five hundred and five one-thousandths
4. ______	4.505	N)	four and five thousand, five hundred and fifty-five ten-thousandths
5. ______	4.005	M)	four and fifty-five one-thousandths
6. ______	4.55	I)	four and five thousand and five ten-thousandths
7. ______	4.5555	S)	four and five one-thousandths

▶ What is the last name of the popular television family?

____

Directions: Read each question carefully. Fill in the bubble next to your answer choice for each question.

1 Which answer is the same as "three and eighteen one-thousandths"?

- ○ A 318
- ○ B 3.18
- ○ C 3.018
- ○ D 3.0018

2 The decimal model below represents the number —

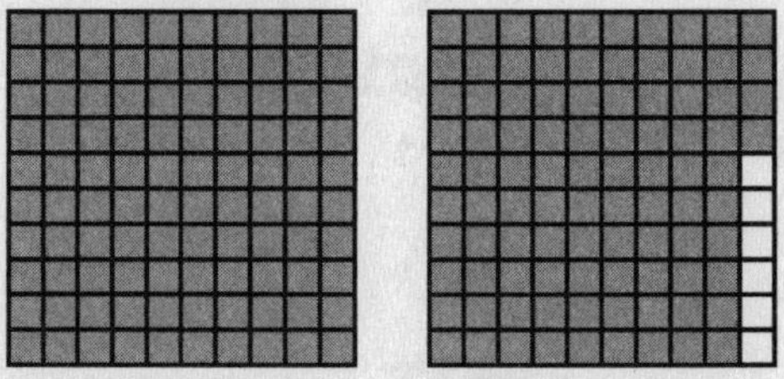

- ○ F 1.94
- ○ G 2.06
- ○ H 3.88
- ○ J 19.4

3 Which phrase is the same as 2.8015?

- ○ A Two thousand, eight hundred and fifteen
- ○ B Two hundred eighty and fifteen ten-thousandths
- ○ C Two and eight hundred fifteen thousandths
- ○ D Two and eight thousand fifteen ten-thousandths

4 Which number does the decimal model represent?

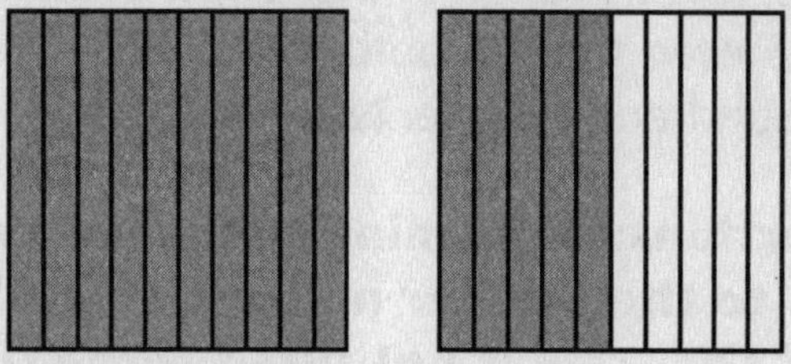

- ○ F 1.05
- ○ G 1.5
- ○ H 1.55
- ○ J 15.5

Most errors on decimal problems involve the number 0. It's easy to put an extra 0 in a decimal. It's also easy to leave out a 0. If you're careful with your 0s, you should have an easy time with decimal problems!

MILE 10: COMPARING DECIMALS

Look at these two numbers: 1.235 and 1.035.

Which one is greater? The number 1.235 is greater because it has a 2 in the tenths place, while 1.035 has a 0 in the tenths place. 2 is greater than 0, so 1.235 is greater than 1.035 even though both numbers begin with 1. Note that the 3s in both numbers are in the hundredths place. Note that the 5s in both numbers are in the thousandths place.

Directions: Determine which number is greater on each scale. If the scale tilts to the greater number, it is tilted correctly. If the scale is correct, circle it. If the scale is not tilted correctly, draw an "X" through it.

1.

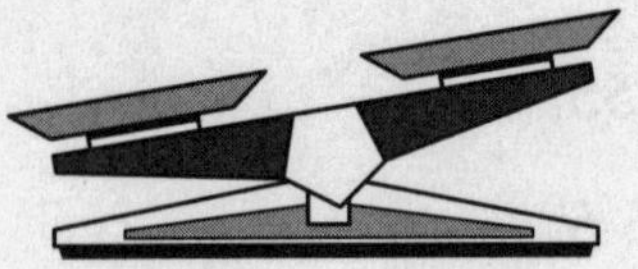

2.049 2.148

2.

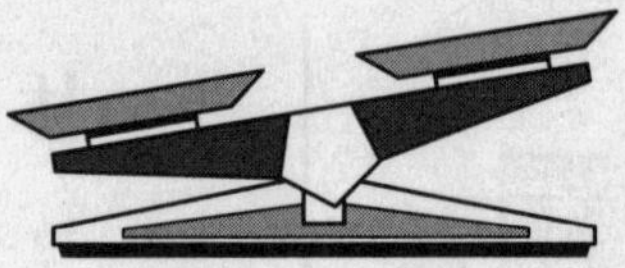

9.86 9.85

3.

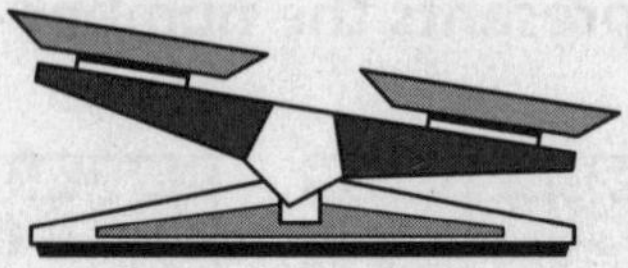

3.021 3.201

4.

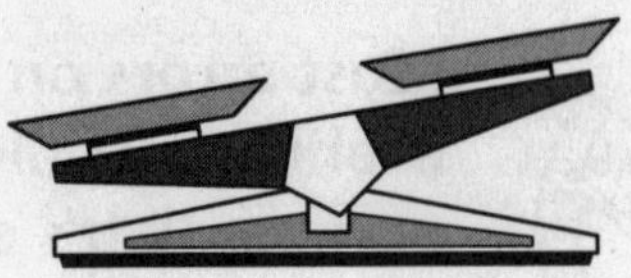

0.0932 0.9002

5.

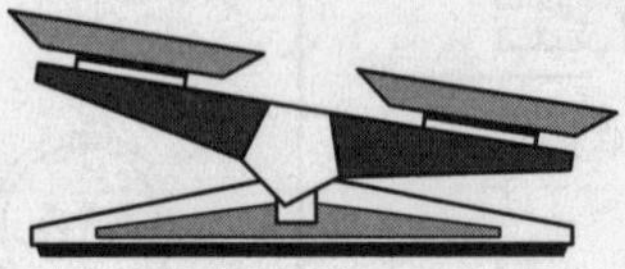

2.333 2.334

6.

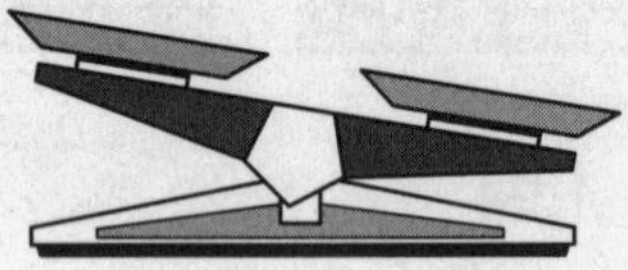

1.9 1.091

7.

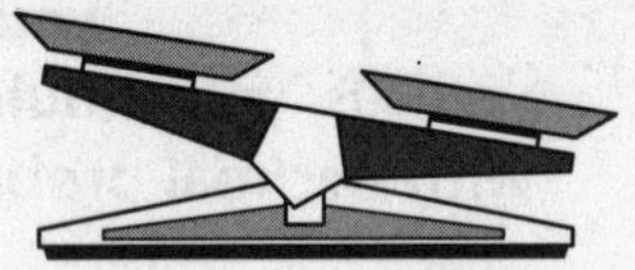

0.01 0.001

8.

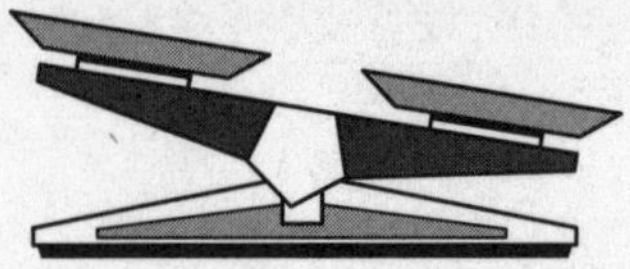

1.001 1.101

9.

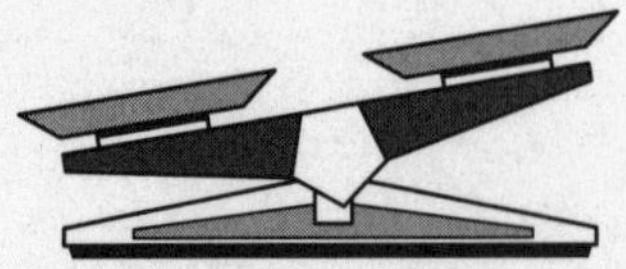

17.72 17.273

10.

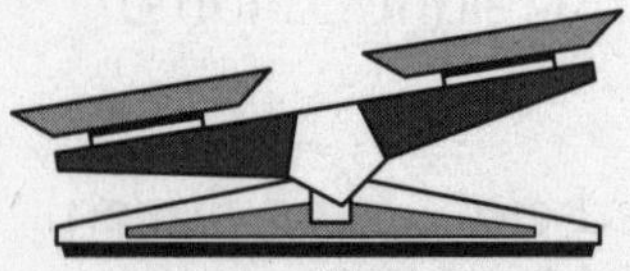

23.254 22.254

Directions: Read each question carefully. Fill in the bubble next to your answer choice for each question.

1 Which statement is true?

- ○ **A** 3.672 > 3.5951
- ○ **B** 3.025 > 3.25
- ○ **C** 3.1416 > 3.152
- ○ **D** 3.1071 > 3.71

2 Which statement is *not* correct?

- ○ **F** 5.141 < 5.2051
- ○ **G** 5.46 = 5.4600
- ○ **H** 5.1705 > 5.182
- ○ **J** 5.328 < 5.4031

3 Which statement is true?

- ○ **A** 8.001 > 8.01
- ○ **B** 8.001 = 8.01
- ○ **C** 8.001 < 8.01
- ○ **D** 8.002 < 8.0002

4 Which statement is *not* true?

- ○ **F** 7.03 = 7.030
- ○ **G** 7.4901 > 7.53
- ○ **H** 7.1 = 7.10
- ○ **J** 7.381 < 7.4021

5 Which statement is correct?

- ○ **A** 2.5 < 2.467
- ○ **B** 2.601 < 2.5888
- ○ **C** 2.4051 < 2.62
- ○ **D** 2.711 < 2.7130

When you compare the values of two decimals, you should always look at the same place values in both decimals. For whole numbers you don't compare the tens place to the ones place. So you shouldn't compare the tenths place to the hundredths place for decimals.

Mile 11: Estimating with Decimals

When you **estimate,** you find a number that is close to the exact amount or number that you're looking for. You can estimate by rounding numbers. A number can be rounded up or down. You round a number up when the number to the right is 5 or greater. You round a number down when the number to the right is less than 5.

You can estimate with decimals by rounding them to the nearest whole number or to the nearest tenth or hundredth. Look at the examples below.

Nearest whole number:	6.2 → 6	4.7 → 5
Nearest tenth:	8.27 → 8.3	13.71 → 13.7
Nearest hundredth:	2.864 → 2.86	51.538 → 51.54

Directions: Help Abigail and her father estimate how much money they will spend on groceries. Also, help them figure out about how much all of their groceries weigh. Estimate all of the numbers by rounding up or down to the nearest tenth. Then answer the questions on the bottom of the page.

Abigail went shopping with her father. They bought five items. Here is the list.

Chicken	3.22 lb. → 3.20 lb.	$4.09 → $4.00
Hamburgers	2.48 lb. → ______	$4.63 → ______
Potatoes	9.83 lb. → ______	$3.84 → ______
Carrots	4.27 lb. → ______	$4.17 → ______
Tomatoes	3.36 lb. → ______	$3.49 → ______

1. Based on your estimations, *about* how much did Abigail and her father spend on groceries?

____

2. Based on your estimations, what is a good estimate for the total weight of their groceries?

____

Directions: Read each question carefully. Fill in the bubble next to your answer choice for each question.

1 A boa constrictor is 3.048 meters long. What is the length of the boa constrictor rounded to the nearest hundredth?

○ A 3.0 meters

○ B 3.04 meters

○ C 3.05 meters

○ D 3.5 meters

2 A drinking glass holds 16.471 fluid ounces. What is the capacity of the drinking glass rounded to the nearest tenth?

○ F 16.5 fluid ounces

○ G 16.48 fluid ounces

○ H 16.47 fluid ounces

○ J 16.4 fluid ounces

3 The temperature in a walk-in freezer is 26.048° F. What is the temperature in the freezer rounded to the nearest tenth?

○ A 25.0° F

○ B 26.0° F

○ C 26.1° F

○ D 30.0° F

4 A professional Sumo wrestler weighs 158.755 kilograms. What is the Sumo wrestler's weight rounded to the nearest hundredth?

○ F 158.8 kilograms

○ G 158.76 kilograms

○ H 158.75 kilograms

○ J 158.7 kilograms

5 A farmer owns 200.138 acres of land. Rounded to the nearest hundredth, how many acres of land does the farmer own?

○ A 200 acres

○ B 200.1 acres

○ C 200.13 acres

○ D 200.14 acres

Estimating with decimals is just as easy as estimating with whole numbers. Don't let the decimal points throw you off. Always look at the number to the right to see if you should round up or down. For example, if you have to round to the nearest tenth, look at the number in the hundredths place (which is to the right of the tenths place). If the number is 5 or greater, round up. If the number is less than 5, round down.

Mile 12: Adding and Subtracting Decimals

You add and subtract decimals just the same way you would with whole numbers. Always remember to line up the decimal points so that tenths are under tenths, hundredths under hundredths, and so on. That's the only way to do it!

Directions: Find the answers in the boxes below and write each letter to the right of the problems in the box that contains its correct answer. The letters will spell out the name of a famous basketball star.

1. $2.367 - 1.943$ (J)
2. $23.54 + 11.32$ (C)
3. $33.98 - 21.72$ (O)
4. $3.43 + 3.43$ (M)
5. $84.6 - 9.5$ (R)
6. $11.10 + 2.91$ (I)
7. $67.02 - 43.12$ (D)
8. $0.739 + 0.151$ (H)
9. $101.3 - 28.2$ (E)
10. $1.79 - 0.81$ (A)
11. $15.35 + 5.65$ (N)
12. $99.027 - 83.026$ (L)
13. $39.746 + 21.222$ (A)

___	___	___	___	___	___	___
6.86	14.01	34.86	0.890	0.98	73.1	16.001

___	___	___	___	___	___
0.424	12.26	75.1	23.90	60.968	21

Directions: Read each question carefully. Fill in the bubble next to your answer choice for each question.

1 Amir has homework almost every night. One week he kept a record of how much time it took to complete his homework.

Day	Time (hours)
Monday	2.2
Tuesday	3.1
Wednesday	2.4
Thursday	1.8
Friday	0 (no homework)

How much time did Amir spend doing his homework last week?

○ **A** 8.15 hours

○ **B** 8.5 hours

○ **C** 9.3 hours

○ **D** 9.5 hours

2 Debra ran the quarter-mile race in 1.33 minutes. Jack ran the same race in 1.46 minutes. How much faster did Debra run the race than Jack?

○ **F** 0.13 minutes

○ **G** 0.16 minutes

○ **H** 1.3 minutes

○ **J** 3.1 minutes

3 At a sporting goods store, tennis balls cost $3.99, a basketball costs $7.49, bike tassels cost $2.59, and a bike helmet costs $6.99. Arlene went to the toy store with $9.00. Which two items can she buy?

○ **A** Basketball and bike tassels

○ **B** Basketball and bike helmet

○ **C** Tennis balls and bike helmet

○ **D** Bike tassels and tennis balls

4
$$\begin{array}{r} 2.3 \\ -\ 0.8 \\ \hline \end{array}$$

○ **F** 1.5

○ **G** 1.4

○ **H** 0.30

○ **J** 0.15

You can always check your answer by doing a quick estimate. Round the numbers to the nearest tenths or hundredths, then add or subtract. If the estimate is close to your exact answer, then there's a good chance that your answer is correct.

Mile 13: Multiplying and Dividing Decimals

To multiply decimals, multiply the same way you multiply whole numbers. Then count the digits to the right of the decimal points in the factors and put a decimal point that many digits from the left in your product. For example, to calculate 3.2×5.4, multiply 32 and 54 to get 1,728. Then place the decimal point two places from the left in your product because there are a total of two decimal places in the factors 3.2 and 5.4. $3.2 \times 5.4 = 17.28$.

To divide by a decimal, use the long division form. If the divisor is a decimal, multiply both the divisor and the dividend by 10, 100, or 1,000 to get rid of the decimal. If the dividend is a decimal, make sure to put a decimal in the quotient right above the decimal in the dividend.

Examples:

To solve $0.6\overline{)3.0}$ multiply both 0.6 and 3.0 by 10. Then solve the problem $30 \div 6$. The answer is 5.0.

To solve $5\overline{)7.5}$ divide as you normally would, but remember to put a decimal point in your quotient directly above the decimal in 7.5.

$$\begin{array}{r} 1.5 \\ 5\overline{)7.5} \end{array}$$

Directions: Solve the decimal problems. Then translate your answers into letters using the code at the bottom of the page. Use the code to fill in the blanks to the right of your answer and you will reveal the secret message.

1. $1.4 \times 21.6 =$ ____ ____ ____ ____

2. $7 \div 3.5 =$ ____

3. $127.9 \times 0.04 =$ ____ ____ ____ ____

4. $14.2 \div 5 =$ ____ ____ ____

5. $4.5119 \times 2 =$ ____ ____ ____ ____ ____

0	1	2	3	4	5	6	7	8	9
E	O	A	R	D	B	K	G	N	L

Directions: Read each question carefully. Fill in the bubble next to your answer choice for each question.

1 $5.7 \times 8.9 =$

- ○ A 14.6
- ○ B 49.63
- ○ C 50.13
- ○ D 50.73

2 $6.76 \div 5 =$

- ○ F 1.1212
- ○ G 1.32
- ○ H 1.352
- ○ J 13.52

3 $2.38 \times 4.3 =$

- ○ A 1.0234
- ○ B 10.234
- ○ C 102.34
- ○ D 1,023.4

4 $0.8\overline{)20}$

- ○ F 2.5
- ○ G 10.25
- ○ H 16
- ○ J 25

5 $10.657 \times 0.4 =$

- ○ A 42.628
- ○ B 14.6
- ○ C 4.2628
- ○ D 2.6645

Multiplying and dividing decimals is almost the same as multiplying and dividing whole numbers. The only difference is that you have to place the decimal point in the correct spot when you are finished with your calculations. If you obey the rules for placing decimals, you should have an easy time answering decimal questions.

MILE 14: MONEY

You can add and subtract money values the same way you add and subtract decimals.

Directions: Each item in the left column has a price tag that contains a number sentence. Solve the number sentence to find the price of the item. Then match the item with its price.

1. ____

2. ____

3. ____

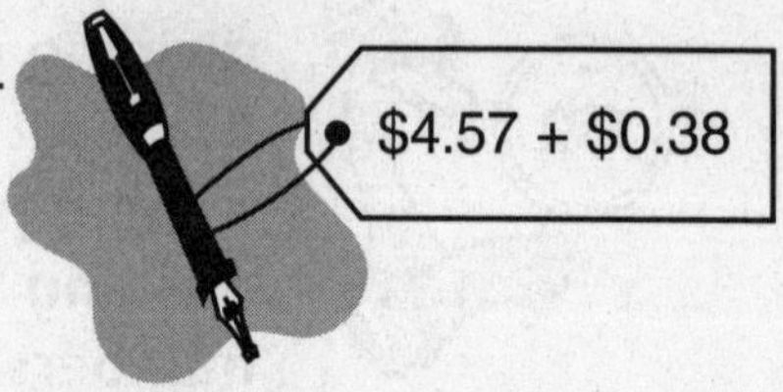

4. ____

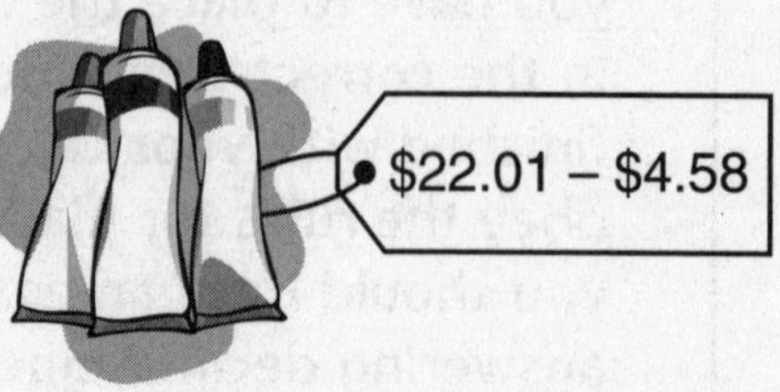

5. ____

A) $4.95

B) $13.79

C) $20.23

D) $3.93

E) $17.43

Directions: Read each question carefully. Fill in the bubble next to your answer choice for each question.

1

Steven has $15 to spend on supplies for his birthday party. If he buys a cake, what else can he buy with the money he has?

○ **A** A board game, a party hat, and three balloons

○ **B** A box of candles, two party hats, and a balloon

○ **C** Two board games and a balloon

○ **D** Two balloons and three party hats

2

Renee bought this box of chocolates. She paid for the box of chocolates with a $20 bill. How much change should the clerk have returned to Renee?

○ **F** $2.42

○ **G** $2.52

○ **H** $12.42

○ **J** $12.52

3

Godfrey has $10.00. Which two items could he buy with the money that he has?

○ **A** A baseball and a bat

○ **B** A glove and a cap

○ **C** A glove and a bat

○ **D** A baseball and a cap

Don't let the dollar and cents signs throw you off. Adding and subtracting money values is exactly the same as adding and subtracting whole numbers or decimals.

MILE 15: FRACTIONS

We're moving on to fractions on our road trip. You should know that a **fraction** is a part of a whole. A fraction has a top number called the **numerator** and a bottom number called the **denominator.** If two fractions have the same denominators, then the fraction with the greater numerator is greater. If two fractions have the same numerators, then the fraction with the lower denominator is greater.

For example, $\frac{3}{4}$ is greater than $\frac{2}{4}$ because 3 is greater than 2.

But, $\frac{2}{4}$ is greater than $\frac{2}{9}$ because 4 is less than 9.

Directions: It's time for a pizza party! Answer the questions below by looking at the picture of the pizza that comes with each one.

1. Janice and her friend LaTanya both like mushrooms on their pizza. If Janice ate $\frac{2}{8}$ of the mushroom pie and LaTanya ate $\frac{3}{8}$, who ate more pizza? ____________

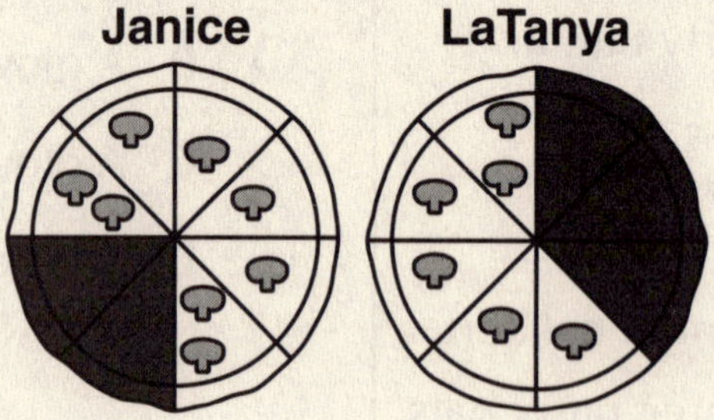

2. What other fraction can you use to show how much of the pizza pie Janice ate? (Hint: Reduce the numerator and denominator.) ____________

3. Janice has an older brother named Freddy who really likes pepperoni. Freddy ordered a whole pepperoni pie for himself. He ate 6 of the 8 slices that came with the pizza. What fraction shows how much of the pepperoni pie he ate? ____________

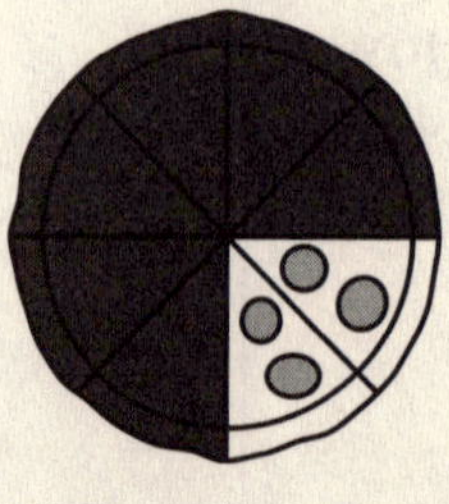

4. What is a simpler way to show how much of the pizza Freddy ate? ____________

Directions: Read each question carefully. Fill in the bubble next to your answer choice for each question.

1 Which of the following is greater than $\frac{5}{8}$?

○ A $\frac{3}{4}$

○ B $\frac{4}{8}$

○ C $\frac{1}{2}$

○ D $\frac{2}{4}$

2 Which fraction has the same value as $\frac{2}{3}$?

○ F $\frac{4}{5}$

○ G $\frac{6}{9}$

○ H $\frac{4}{9}$

○ J $\frac{2}{6}$

3 Which of the following sets of fractions contains all fractions that are equal to each other?

○ A $\frac{4}{5}, \frac{8}{10}, \frac{10}{15}$

○ B $\frac{3}{8}, \frac{6}{16}, \frac{12}{32}$

○ C $\frac{2}{8}, \frac{3}{4}, \frac{4}{16}$

○ D $\frac{2}{7}, \frac{4}{14}, \frac{7}{21}$

4 Jim has four packages to mail. Which two packages have the same weight?

1	2	3	4
$1\frac{2}{3}$ lb.	$\frac{3}{4}$ lb.	$1\frac{3}{4}$ lb.	$1\frac{4}{6}$ lb.

○ F 1 and 4

○ G 1 and 3

○ H 2 and 3

○ J 3 and 4

5 Alex, Maggie, Jules, and Dottie are all baking cookies for the county fair. Alex's recipe calls for $1\frac{2}{3}$ cups of flour. Maggie's recipe calls for $1\frac{3}{4}$ cups. Jules's recipe calls for $1\frac{1}{3}$ cups. Dottie's recipe calls for 1 1\5 cups. Whose recipe requires the most flour?

○ A Alex's

○ B Maggie's

○ C Jules's

○ D Dottie's

If two fractions have the same numerator (top number), the fraction with the greater denominator (bottom number) has a smaller value. This is easy to understand when you think of a cake. You get more cake if you split it 8 ways rather than 10 ways. If you split it 8 ways, you get $\frac{1}{8}$ of the cake. If you split it 10 ways, you get $\frac{1}{10}$ of the cake. So you know that $\frac{1}{8}$ is greater than $\frac{1}{10}$.

Mile 16: Equivalent Fractions

Fractions are equal when they represent the same part of a whole. To find out whether fractions are equal, rewrite the fractions so that they have the same denominator. If they also have the same numerator, then they are equal!

Example:

Are $\frac{1}{2}$ and $\frac{2}{4}$ equal? To find out, write them so that they have the same denominator. Multiply $\frac{1}{2}$ by $\frac{2}{2}$ to rewrite $\frac{1}{2}$ as $\frac{1}{2} \times \frac{2}{2} = \frac{2}{4}$. Are $\frac{2}{4}$ and $\frac{2}{4}$ equal? Yes, so $\frac{1}{2}$ and $\frac{2}{4}$ are equal.

Directions: The following boxes each contain two fractions and a letter. Find the boxes that contain equivalent fractions. Start with the top row going from left to right. When you get to the end of the first row, start at the beginning of the second row. Cross out the boxes that do not contain equivalent fractions. When you are done, copy the remaining letters in order into the blanks at the bottom of the page to learn the answer to the riddle.

I $\frac{1}{3}$ $\frac{3}{9}$	**V** $\frac{3}{4}$ $\frac{3}{8}$	**N** $\frac{2}{5}$ $\frac{4}{10}$	**Y** $\frac{2}{3}$ $\frac{4}{10}$	**A** $\frac{1}{5}$ $\frac{2}{5}$
C $\frac{1}{6}$ $\frac{1}{9}$	**H** $\frac{1}{2}$ $\frac{3}{6}$	**R** $\frac{1}{4}$ $\frac{4}{8}$	**I** $\frac{3}{4}$ $\frac{9}{12}$	**S** $\frac{1}{3}$ $\frac{2}{6}$
B $\frac{1}{6}$ $\frac{4}{9}$	**B** $\frac{1}{3}$ $\frac{3}{10}$	**S** $\frac{2}{3}$ $\frac{4}{6}$	**O** $\frac{1}{4}$ $\frac{2}{12}$	**L** $\frac{1}{5}$ $\frac{2}{10}$
W $\frac{1}{3}$ $\frac{2}{5}$	**E** $\frac{1}{6}$ $\frac{2}{12}$	**E** $\frac{1}{4}$ $\frac{2}{8}$	**K** $\frac{1}{5}$ $\frac{4}{8}$	**V** $\frac{1}{2}$ $\frac{6}{12}$
I $\frac{4}{5}$ $\frac{8}{10}$	**N** $\frac{3}{4}$ $\frac{5}{8}$	**E** $\frac{1}{4}$ $\frac{2}{8}$	**S** $\frac{1}{4}$ $\frac{3}{12}$	**D** $\frac{2}{3}$ $\frac{2}{6}$

▶ Where did the general keep his armies?

____ ____   ____ ____ ____

____ ____ ____ ____ ____ ____ ____ ____

Directions: Read each question carefully. Fill in the bubble next to your answer choice for each question.

1 **A fraction of these mittens is shaded.**

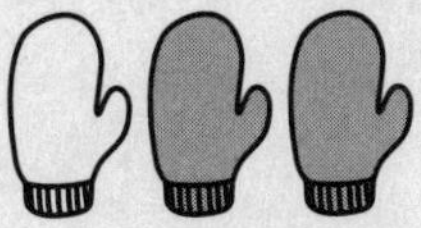

Which answer shows mittens with an equivalent fraction shaded?

○ **A** 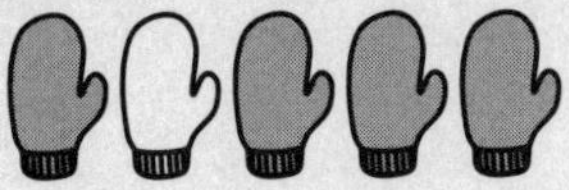

○ **B** 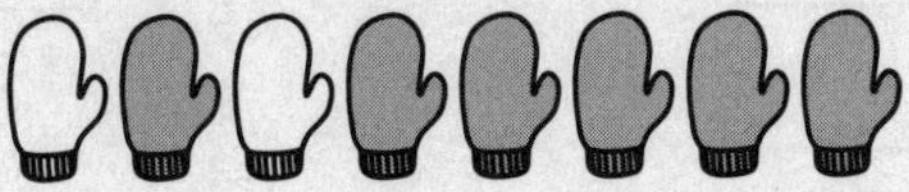

○ **C** 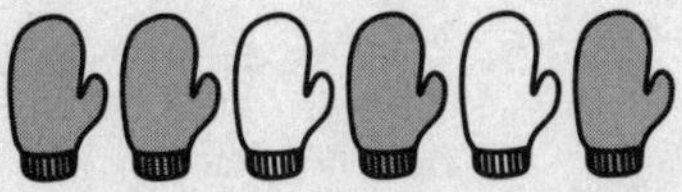

○ **D** 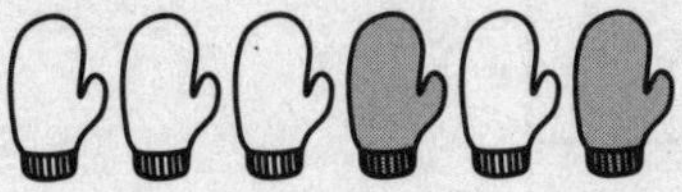

2 **A fraction of this rectangle is shaded.**

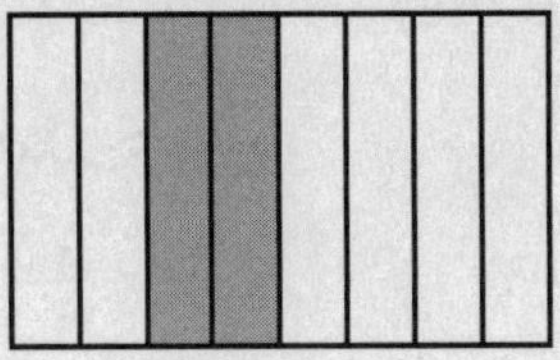

Which rectangle has an equivalent fraction shaded?

○ **F** 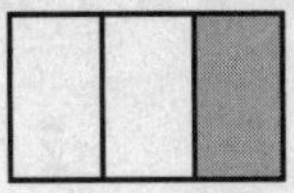

○ **G** 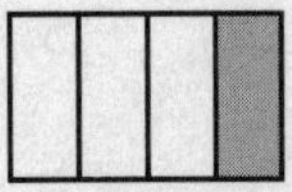

○ **H** 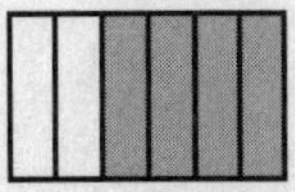

○ **J** 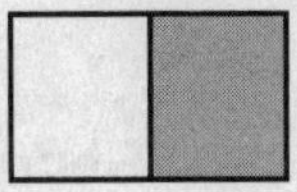

You can determine whether fractions are equivalent using cross-multiplication. Multiply the denominator of each fraction by the numerator of the other. If the products are equal, you'll know that the fractions are equal.

Example: $\frac{2}{3} \times \frac{4}{6}$ **$3 \times 4 = 12$ and $6 \times 2 = 12$, so $\frac{2}{3}$ and $\frac{4}{6}$ are equivalent fractions.**

MILE 17: ADDING AND SUBTRACTING FRACTIONS

Adding and subtracting fractions isn't very difficult. When you add or subtract fractions with the same denominators (bottom numbers), the denominator in the answer stays the same. You only have to add or subtract the numerators (top numbers).

Example 1:

$\frac{3}{4} + \frac{1}{4} = \frac{4}{4} = 1$

Example 2:

$\frac{3}{4} - \frac{1}{4} = \frac{2}{4} = \frac{1}{2}$

Directions: Answer each problem below. When you find an answer, check the Secret Code Breaker and copy the letter that matches the answer into the numbered boxes. When you finish all of the questions, the numbered boxes will spell the name of a U.S. president.

1. $\frac{5}{9} - \frac{3}{9} =$ ______
2. $\frac{2}{3} + \frac{1}{3} =$ ______
3. $\frac{7}{19} - \frac{3}{19} =$ ______
4. $\frac{2}{7} + \frac{3}{7} =$ ______
5. $\frac{9}{21} - \frac{5}{21} =$ ______
6. $\frac{8}{19} + \frac{5}{19} =$ ______
7. $\frac{1}{2} - \frac{1}{2} =$ ______
8. $3\frac{3}{8} + \frac{4}{8} =$ ______
9. $\frac{13}{21} - \frac{8}{21} =$ ______
10. $\frac{3}{8} + \frac{3}{8} =$ ______
11. $\frac{12}{29} - \frac{7}{29} =$ ______
12. $\frac{13}{14} - \frac{7}{14} =$ ______
13. $7\frac{5}{9} - \frac{1}{9} =$ ______
14. $\frac{2}{3} - \frac{1}{3} =$ ______
15. $\frac{9}{10} - \frac{1}{10} =$ ______

Secret Code Breaker

V $\frac{5}{7}$	A $7\frac{4}{9}$	G $\frac{2}{9}$	E $\frac{4}{21}$	O $\frac{4}{19}$
C 0	R 1	E $\frac{5}{21}$	L $3\frac{7}{8}$	E $\frac{5}{29}$
R $\frac{13}{19}$	N $\frac{1}{3}$	V $\frac{3}{4}$	L $\frac{3}{7}$	D $\frac{4}{5}$

► Who was both the 22nd and 24th U.S. president?

1	2	3	4	5	6
___	___	___	___	___	___

7	8	9	10	11	12	13	14	15
___	___	___	___	___	___	___	___	___

Directions: Read each question carefully. Fill in the bubble next to your answer choice for each question.

1

$$\begin{array}{r} 4\frac{2}{5} \\ -\ \frac{1}{5} \\ \hline \end{array}$$

○ A $4\frac{4}{5}$

○ B $4\frac{3}{5}$

○ C $4\frac{1}{5}$

○ D $\frac{1}{5}$

2 If you subtract the gray shaded parts from the figure below, how much of the figure will be left?

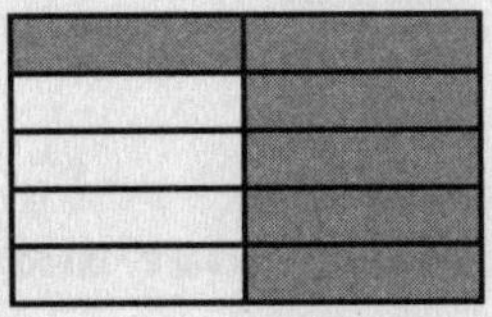

○ F $\frac{3}{12}$

○ G $\frac{2}{5}$

○ H $\frac{7}{10}$

○ J 4

3

$$\begin{array}{r} \frac{1}{6} \\ +\ \frac{5}{6} \\ \hline \end{array}$$

○ A 0

○ B $\frac{1}{6}$

○ C $\frac{2}{3}$

○ D 1

4 What is the answer to this problem?

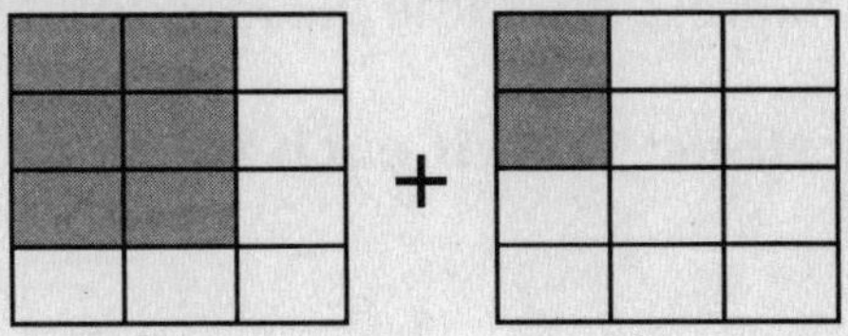

○ F 8

○ G $\frac{12}{12}$

○ H $\frac{8}{12}$

○ J $\frac{3}{6}$

Sometimes fractions in answer choices are reduced to lowest terms. Other times they are not. Always check each answer choice carefully.

MILE 18: COMPARING DECIMALS AND FRACTIONS

All fractions can be written as decimals. The numbers $\frac{3}{10}$ and 0.30 may look different, but they express the same value. Another example is $\frac{64}{100} = 0.64$.

Directions: Match each fraction with the correct decimal.

1. _____	$\frac{1}{5}$	A)	0.25
2. _____	$\frac{1}{4}$	B)	0.75
3. _____	$\frac{4}{10}$	C)	0.40
4. _____	$\frac{80}{100}$	D)	0.20
5. _____	$\frac{15}{25}$	E)	0.60
6. _____	$\frac{9}{12}$	F)	0.80

Directions: Answer each of the following questions. Write your answers on the lines provided.

7.

You found 33 cents on the sidewalk. Expressed as a fraction and a decimal, how much of dollar is this? ____________, ____________

8. Susie's allowance each week is $10. By Wednesday she had already spent $6. How much does she have left? Express your answer first as a fraction, then as a decimal.

____________, ____________

9. It took Julie $\frac{4}{5}$ of an hour to do last night's homework. Armando did the same homework in 0.85 hours. Who did it faster? ____________

Directions: Read each question carefully. Fill in the bubble next to your answer choice for each question.

1 What is 0.5 expressed as a fraction?

○ A $\frac{1}{2}$

○ B $\frac{2}{3}$

○ C $\frac{3}{4}$

○ D $\frac{4}{5}$

2 Which point on the number line represents the number $2\frac{3}{6}$?

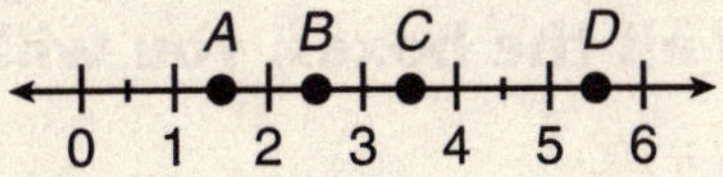

○ F *A*

○ G *B*

○ H *C*

○ J *D*

3 Which of the following numbers is greater than $1\frac{4}{5}$?

○ A 0.95

○ B 1.90

○ C $1\frac{7}{10}$

○ D $1\frac{6}{9}$

4 Omar had a great idea. He wanted to recycle paper and make some money for his after-school club. The club members agreed. For each bundle of old newspapers the club members collected, they received $\frac{3}{5}$ of a dollar. Expressed as a decimal, how much did the club receive for each bundle of newspapers?

○ F $0.35

○ G $0.50

○ H $0.60

○ J $0.75

It is easy to convert a fraction to a decimal on your calculator. For example, suppose you want to convert $\frac{2}{5}$ to a decimal. Just type in 2 ÷ 5 and—***Abracadabra!***—you get 0.4.

MILE 19: PERIMETER

The distance around a figure is called the **perimeter.** Because it is a distance, perimeter is measured in inches, feet, centimeters, or meters. Look at the example below.

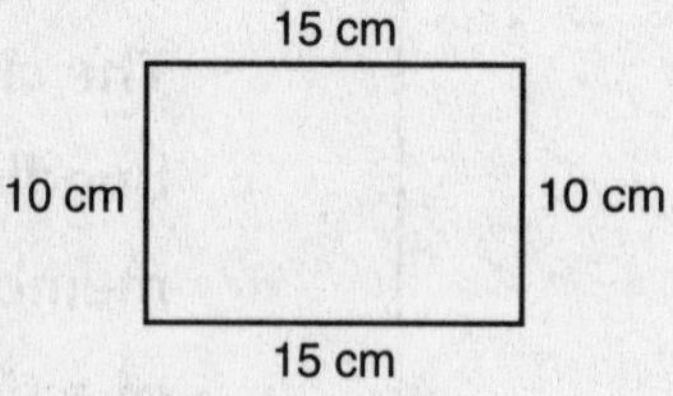

It's easy to find the perimeter of the rectangle above. Just add up the lengths of all the sides: 10 cm + 10 cm + 15 cm + 15 cm = 50 cm. The perimeter of the rectangle is 50 cm.

Directions: Find the perimeters of these six objects. Write your answer on the line provided. Then fill in the letter in the box at the bottom of the page that matches the answer it goes with. When you fill in all the boxes, you will have the answer to the riddle below.

▶ What type of bird can lift the most?

1.

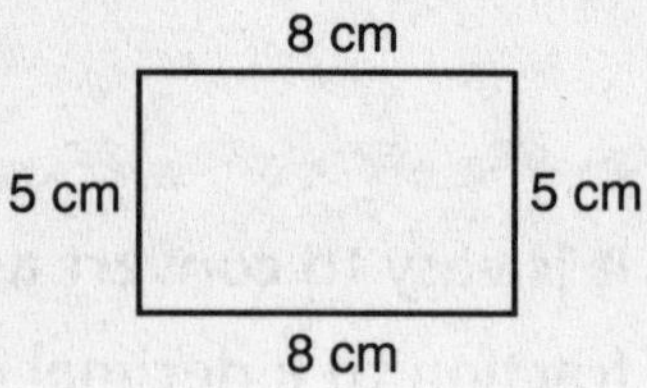

______ = N

2.

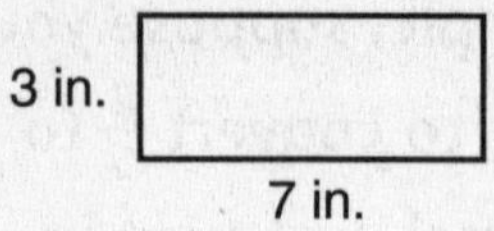

______ = A

3.

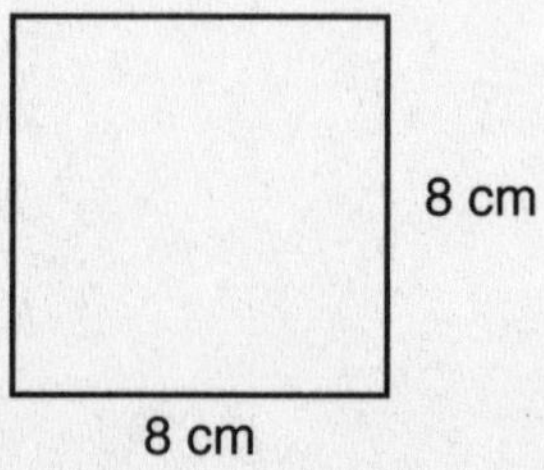

______ = E

4.

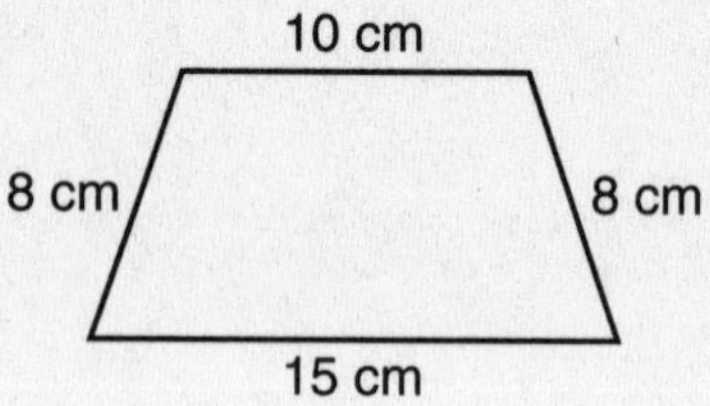

______ = R

5.

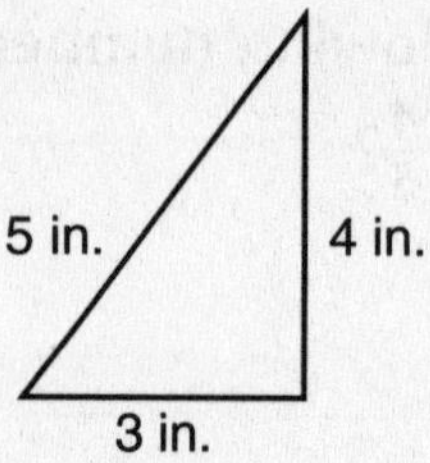

______ = C

Answer:

___	___	___	___	___
12 in.	41 cm	20 in.	26 cm	32 cm

Directions: Read each question carefully. Fill in the bubble next to your answer choice for each question.

1 What is the perimeter of this T-shaped figure?

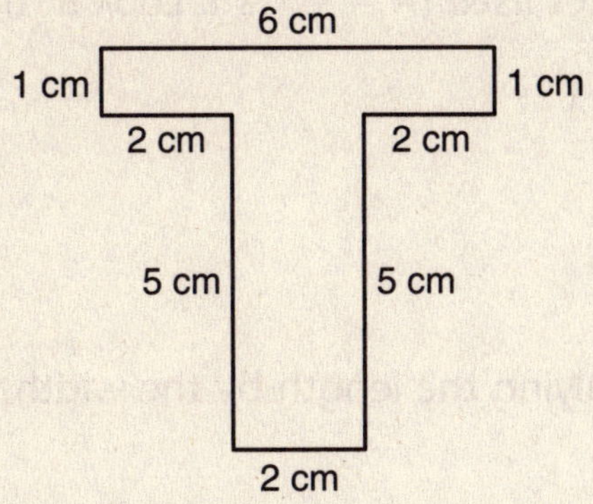

○ **A** 15 centimeters

○ **B** 18 centimeters

○ **C** 20 centimeters

○ **D** 24 centimeters

2 You will need to use your inch ruler to answer this question. The perimeter of this square is most nearly —

○ **F** 4 inches

○ **G** 5 inches

○ **H** 6 inches

○ **J** 8 inches

3 The perimeter of this figure is most nearly —

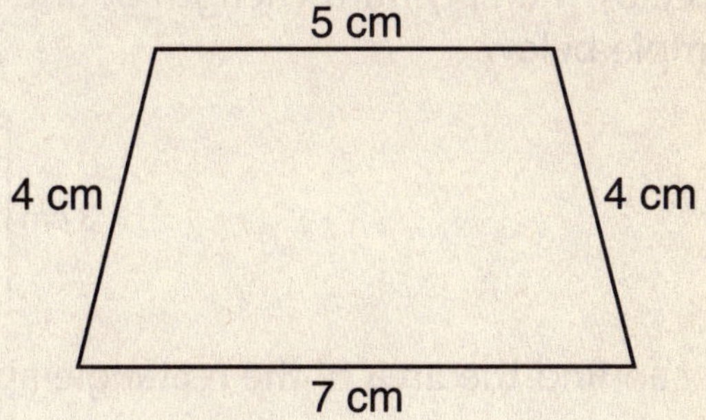

○ **A** 28 centimeters

○ **B** 20 centimeters

○ **C** 9 centimeters

○ **D** 8 centimeters

You can take a shortcut to find the perimeter of a square. You know that the lengths of all four sides of a square are equal. So all you have to do to get the perimeter is multiply the length of one side by 4.

MILE 20: AREA

The **area** of a figure is how much surface the figure covers. You can find the area of a *rectangle* by multiplying its length times its width ($A = l \times w$). You can find the area of a *square* by multiplying the length of one of its sides times itself ($A = s \times s$). Look at the example below.

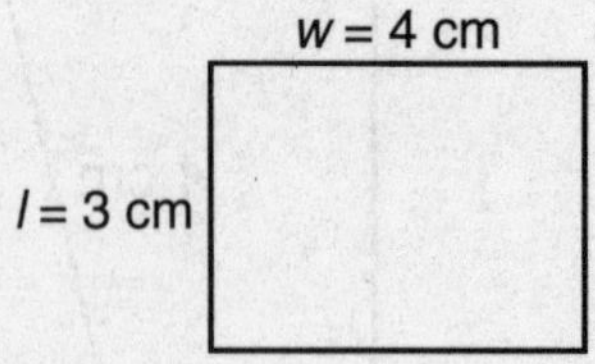

You can find the area of the rectangle above by multiplying the length by the width.

$$A = 3 \times 4 = 12 \text{ cm}^2$$

Directions: Find the area of the objects shaped like squares or rectangles. Don't forget the units!

1.

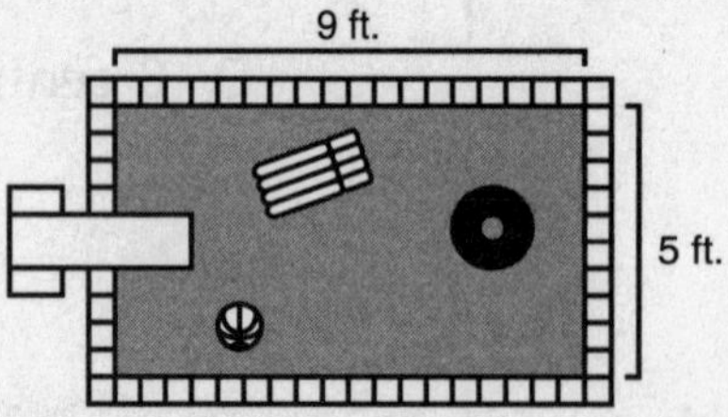

What is the area of the swimming pool? ____________

2.

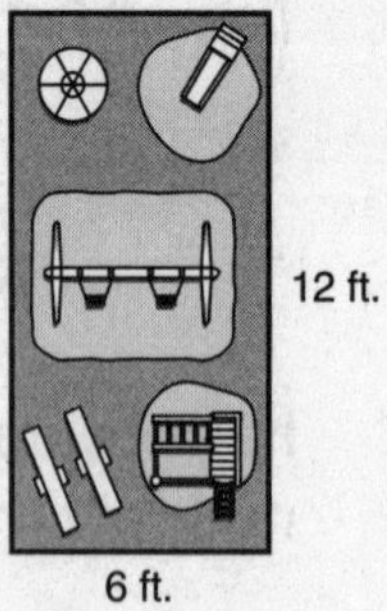

What is the area of the playground? ____________

3.

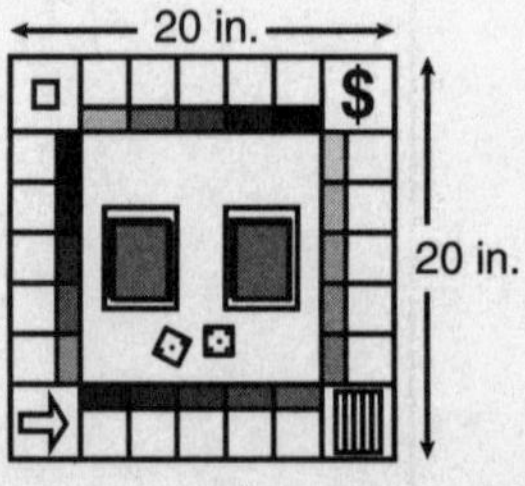

What is the area of the board game? ____________

Directions: Read each question carefully. Fill in the bubble next to your answer choice for each question.

1 Jake and his mother plan to put wall-to-wall carpeting in their living room. If the dimensions of the living room are 14 feet by 20 feet, how much carpeting do they need?

○ **A** 34 $feet^2$

○ **B** 140 $feet^2$

○ **C** 280 $feet^2$

○ **D** 340 $feet^2$

2 Which of the following expressions will give you the area of the rectangle below?

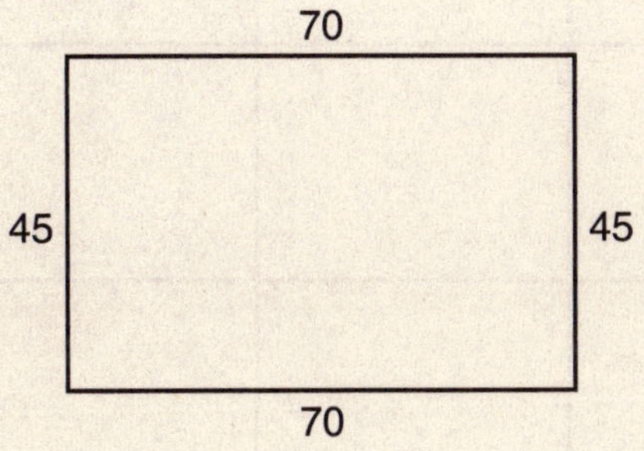

○ **F** $70 \times 70 \times 45 \times 45$

○ **G** 70×45

○ **H** $70 + 70 + 45 + 45$

○ **J** $70 \times 70 + 45$

3 If the area of a square is 100 cm^2, what is the length of any one side?

○ **A** 25 centimeters

○ **B** 20 centimeters

○ **C** 15 centimeters

○ **D** 10 centimeters

4 A rectangle with a width of 5 inches and a length of 6 inches has an area of —

○ **F** 10 $inches^2$

○ **G** 11 $inches^2$

○ **H** 22 $inches^2$

○ **J** 30 $inches^2$

Area is measured in square units such as cm^2 (read "centimeters squared") or ft^2 (read "square feet"). Get rid of all answer choices that do not show square units with questions that ask for the area of a figure.

Mile 21: Using Area and Perimeter

The perimeter of any shape is found by adding the lengths of its sides.
The area of a rectangle is found by multiplying the length and the width.

Directions: Each of the following figures is a rectangle made up of squares. Use these squares to determine the perimeter and the area of each rectangle. Write the perimeter and area in the appropriate spaces to the right of each shape. Use the code at the bottom of the page to translate the perimeters and areas into letters. Then fill in the letters in the space provided on the right side of the page. Read the columns vertically to discover the name of a delicious food.

	Perimeter	Area	Perimeter Code Letter	Area Code Letter
1. 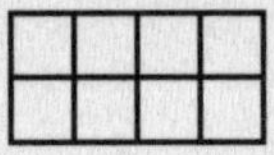				
2. 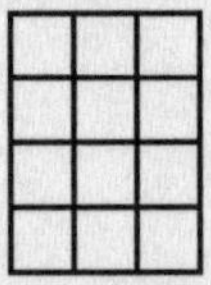				
3. 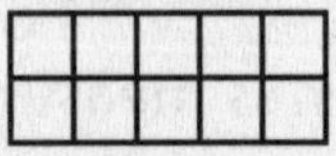				
4. 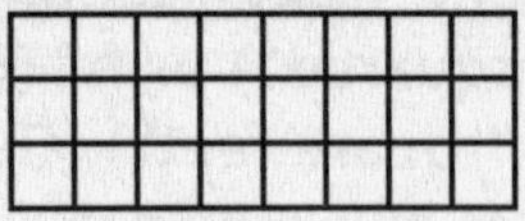				
5. 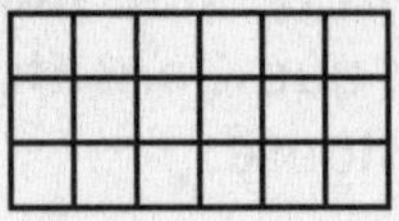				

1 = H	2 = M	3 = B	4 = O	5 = R	6 = N	7 = F	8 = S	9 = G	10 = U
11 = Q	12 = A	13 = J	14 = P	15 = T	16 = W	17 = Z	18 = E	19 = Y	20 = D
21 = I	22 = L	23 = X	24 = C	25 = V	26 = K				

► What is the name of the delicious food?

_____ _____ _____ _____ _____   _____ _____ _____ _____ _____

Directions: Read each question carefully. Fill in the bubble next to your answer choice for each question.

1 Which question can only be answered by figuring out the area of something?

- ○ **A** How much carpet is needed to cover a floor?
- ○ **B** How many number cubes will fit into a box?
- ○ **C** How much ribbon is needed to wrap a package?
- ○ **D** How many inches tall is a flagpole?

2 Which figure has an area of 20?

○ **F** 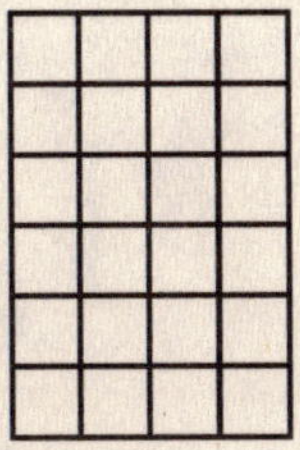

○ **G** 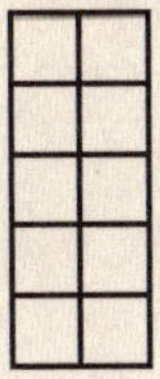

○ **H** 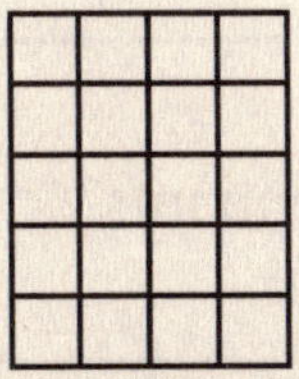

○ **J** 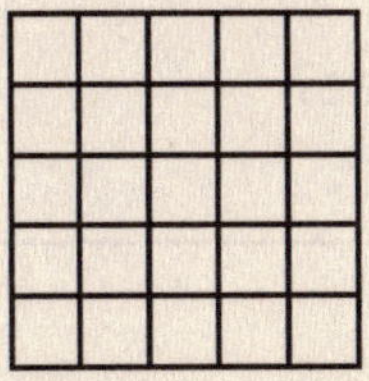

3 Mr. Valdez wants to build a fence around his swimming pool. To know how much fencing he needs to buy, he will have to know the —

- ○ **A** volume of the swimming pool
- ○ **B** perimeter of the swimming pool
- ○ **C** depth of the swimming pool
- ○ **D** area of the swimming pool

4 Which figure has a perimeter of 12?

○ **F** 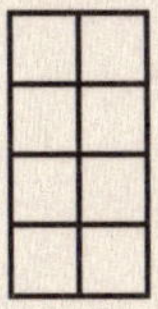

○ **G** 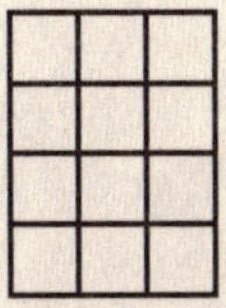

○ **H** 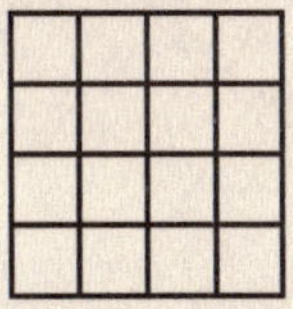

○ **J** 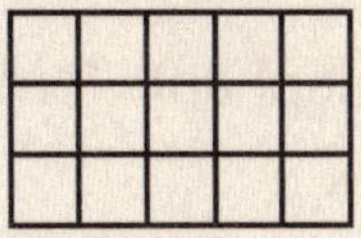

Do all your work on scratch paper, not in your head. It is especially important to write down all your work when you are calculating two numbers such as area and perimeter. Write clearly and carefully so you know the purpose of each calculation.

MILE 22: CIRCLES

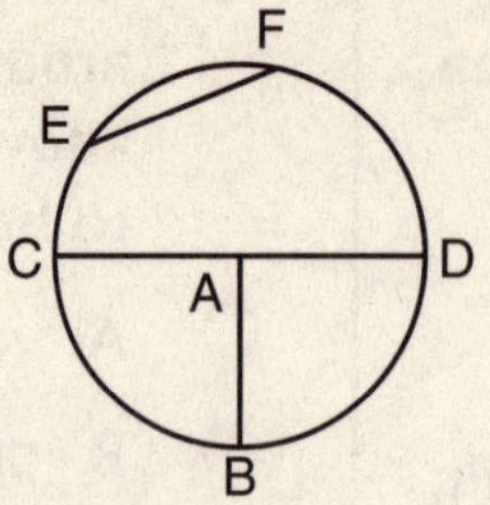

Point *A* is the center of the circle. Line segment $\overline{AB}$ is a radius. Line segment $\overline{CAD}$, which is twice as long as $\overline{AB}$, is a diameter. Line segment $\overline{EF}$ is a chord.

Directions: It's time to stop off at the circus on our road trip! Check out the three-ring circus and then answer the questions below it.

1. What do the elephants form in the center ring?

____

2. At what point in the ring is the ringmaster standing with the elephants?

____

3. In the left ring what do the acrobats form on the flying trapeze?

____

4. What is formed by the clowns in the ring on the right?

____

Directions: Read each question carefully. Fill in the bubble next to your answer choice for each question.

1 If the radius of a circle is 24 centimeters, what is its diameter?

○ **A** 72 centimeters

○ **B** 48 centimeters

○ **C** 36 centimeters

○ **D** 15 centimeters

2 A circle has a diameter of 6 inches. What is its radius?

○ **F** 12 inches

○ **G** 9 inches

○ **H** 6 inches

○ **J** 3 inches

3 Which of these statements is false?

○ **A** A radius has a point on the center of a circle.

○ **B** A diameter has a point on the center of a circle.

○ **C** A chord always has a point on the center of a circle.

○ **D** There can be more than one radius on a circle.

4 What is the correct name for line segment $\overline{AB}$ in the circle below?

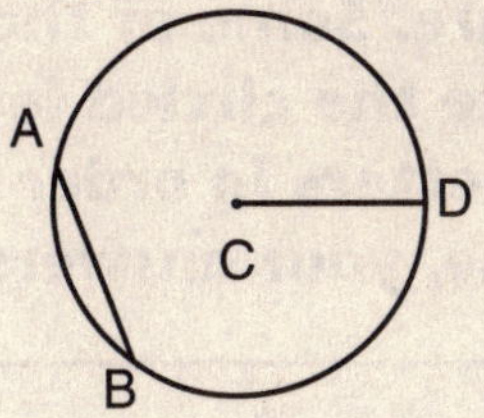

○ **F** Area

○ **G** Chord

○ **H** Radius

○ **J** Diameter

Always remember that the diameter of a circle is twice as long as the radius. The radius is half as long as the diameter.

Mile 23: Points, Lines, Segments, and Rays

Directions: Look at the words in the box. Then read the incomplete statements that follow. Write the appropriate word in the blanks to the right of each figure. Some of the blanks are circled. After you have filled in all the blanks, write the circled letters in the blanks at the bottom of the page. Copy the circled letters in order from top to bottom and from left to right. When you are done, your answers will spell out the names of two countries.

intersect	segment	perpendicular	ray
line	parallel	point	

1. 
The illustration shows a _ (_)(_) _.

2. 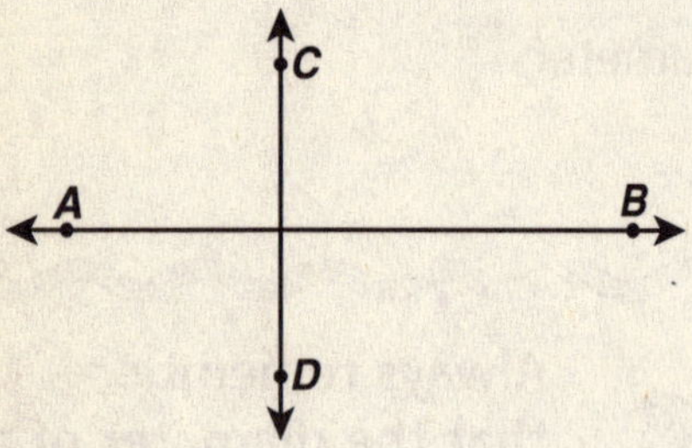
The line segments in the illustration are _ _ _ _ _ _ (_)(_) _ _ _ _ _.

3. 
The figure shows a _ (_) _.

4. 
The figure shows a line (_) _ _ _ _ _ _.

5. 
The figure shows a (_) _ _ _ _.

6. 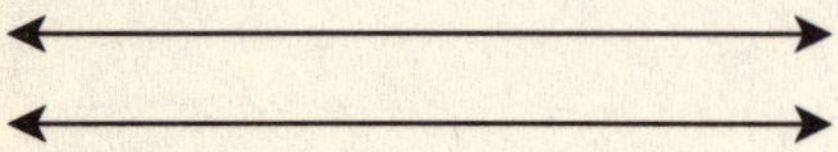
The lines shown on the left are _ (_) _ _ _ _ _ _.

7. 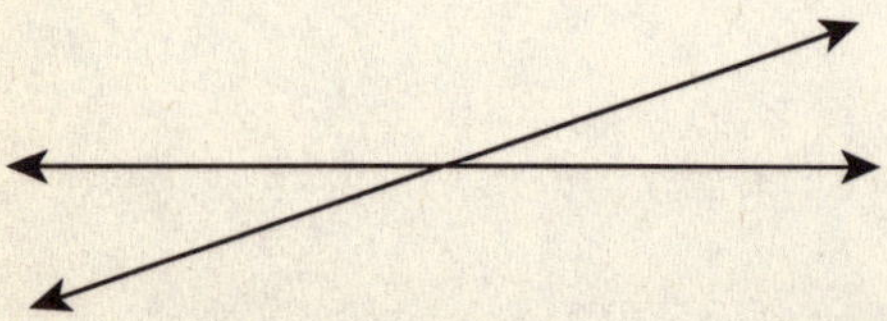
These two lines (_)(_) _ _ _ _ _ _ _.

► **What are the two countries?** ***Country #1:*** | | | | | |

Country #2: | | | | | |

Directions: Read each question carefully. Fill in the bubble next to your answer choice for each question.

1 **Which figure shows a ray?**

○ A 

○ B 

○ C 

○ D 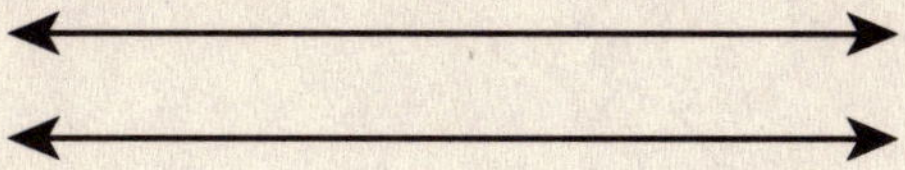

2 **Parallel lines —**

○ **F** meet at right corners

○ **G** intersect more than once

○ **H** never meet

○ **J** have endpoints

3 **Perpendicular lines form four —**

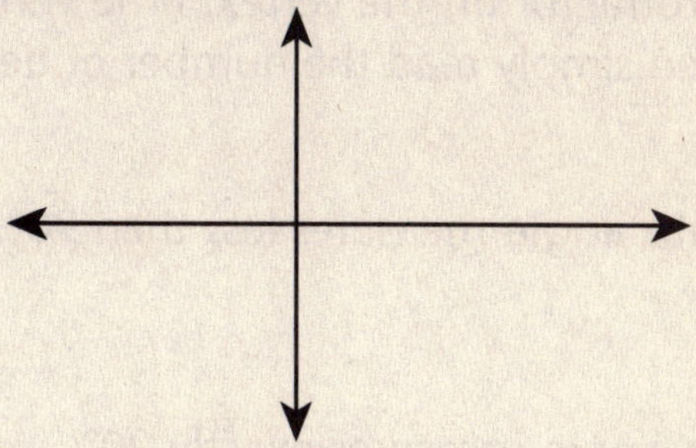

○ **A** intersections

○ **B** right angles

○ **C** line segments

○ **D** parallel lines

Study the names of all the different geometric figures. If you don't know what certain terms mean, such as *angle, ray,* and *line segment,* you cannot answer questions about them. Make flash cards for each term you don't know and study the cards until you know every important geometry term by heart.

Mile 24: Angles

You can measure an **angle** by laying a protractor along one of the rays and lining up your protractor on the vertex. (The vertex is the point at which the two rays meet.) You then simply read the number of degrees off the protractor.

An **acute angle** measures less than 90°.

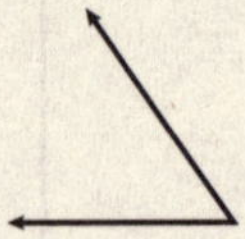

A **right angle** measures exactly 90°.

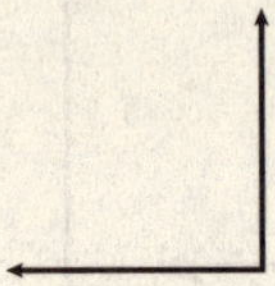

An **obtuse angle** measures more than 90°.

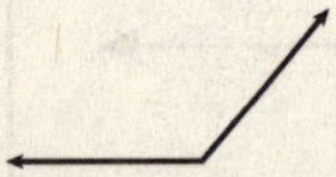

Directions: For each angle below identify its type (acute, right, or obtuse). Then estimate the angle's measurement without using a protractor—just use your eye. After you estimate its measurement, get a protractor to get an exact measurement of the angle. If you need to, draw a line that connects the ray of the angle to the measurement on your protractor. Then compare the measurement of the protractor with your guess. How close are you?

1. 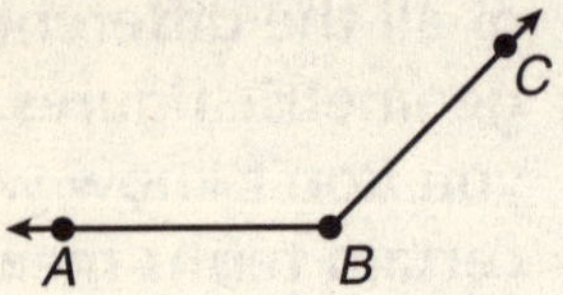

Type: ________ Estimate: ________ Protractor: ________

2. 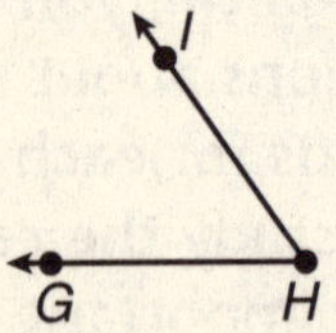

Type: ________ Estimate: ________ Protractor: ________

3. 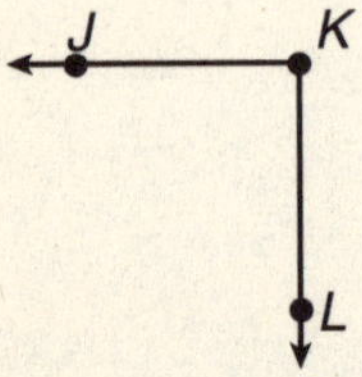

Type: ________ Estimate: ________ Protractor: ________

4. 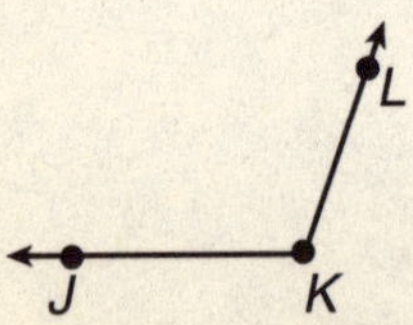

Type: ________ Estimate: ________ Protractor: ________

Directions: Read each question carefully. Fill in the bubble next to your answer choice for each question.

1 Which one of these is an acute angle?

○ **A**

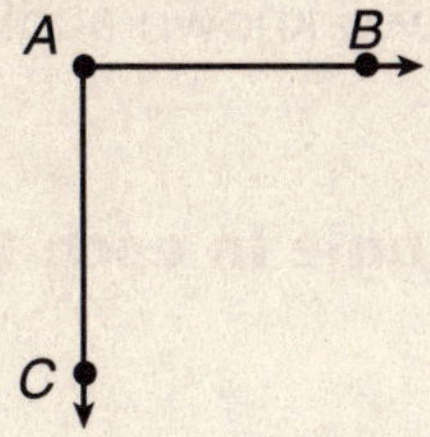

○ **B**

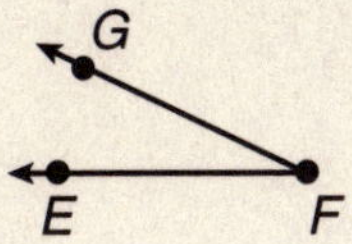

○ **C**

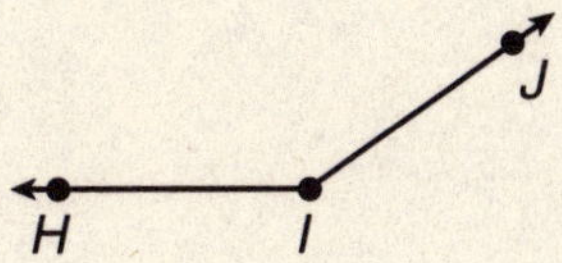

○ **D**

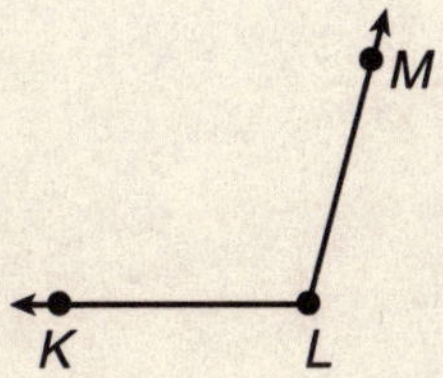

2 ∠*XZY* is what type of angle?

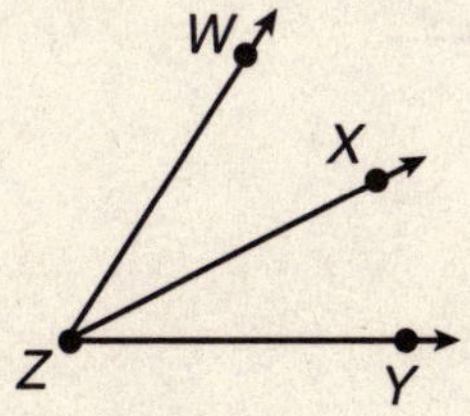

○ **F** Acute angle

○ **G** Obtuse angle

○ **H** Right angle

○ **J** Exterior angle

3 Which of the following is the best estimate for the measurement of ∠*ACD*?

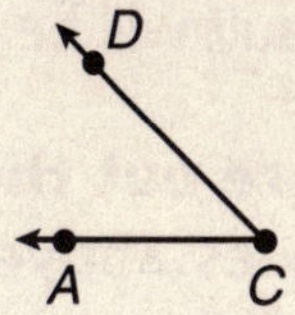

○ **A** 45°

○ **B** 90°

○ **C** 135°

○ **D** 180°

4 What is the best estimate of the measurement of ∠*ACB*?

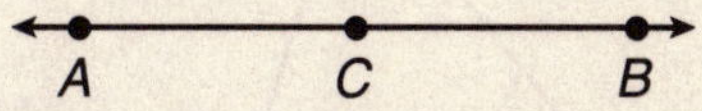

○ **F** 0°

○ **G** 90°

○ **H** 180°

○ **J** 270°

To remember what an acute angle is, think of the word *cute.* Something that is cute is usually small. An acute angle is the smallest of the three types of angles—it is less than 90°.

MILE 25: TRIANGLES

The three angles inside a triangle add up to 180°. This is true for *all* triangles. If you know the measurements of two of the angles, you can easily figure out the measurement of the third angle. All you have to do is subtract the measurements for the two known angles from 180°. The result will be the measurement of the unknown angle.

Directions: Figure out the measurement of the unknown angle in each triangle based on the rules above.

1.

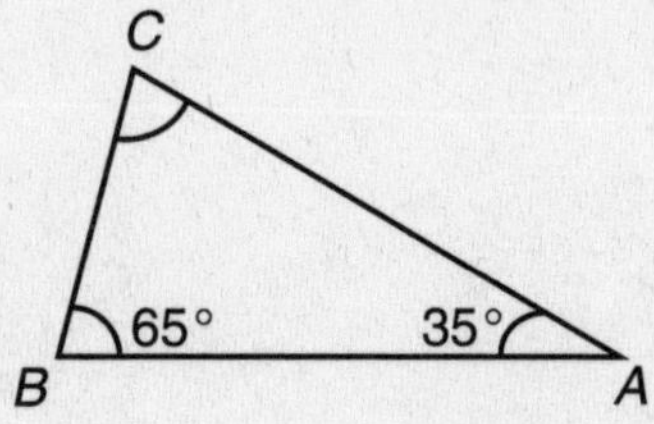

∠C: ________

2.

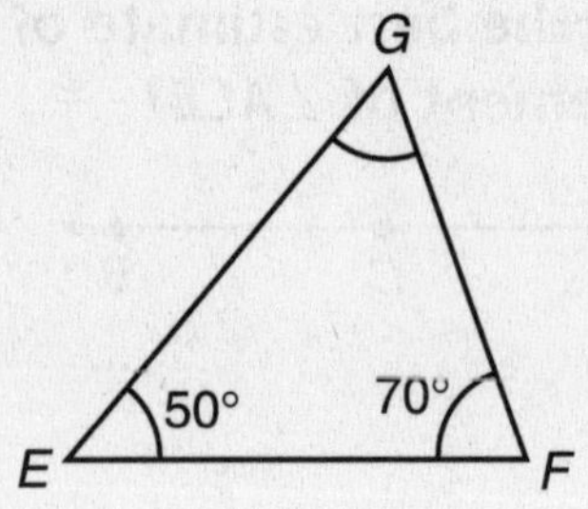

∠G: ________

3.

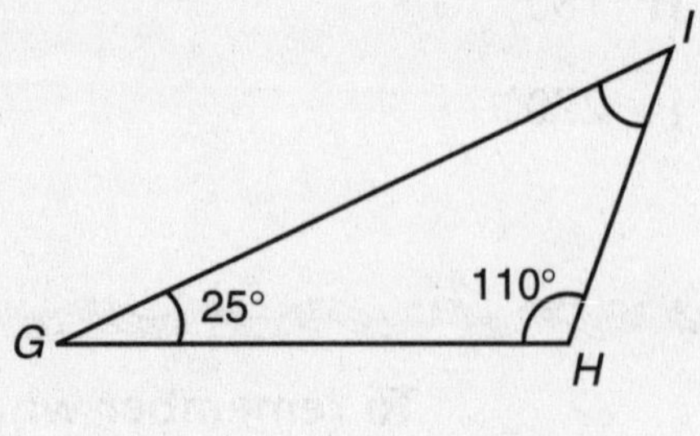

∠I: ________

4.

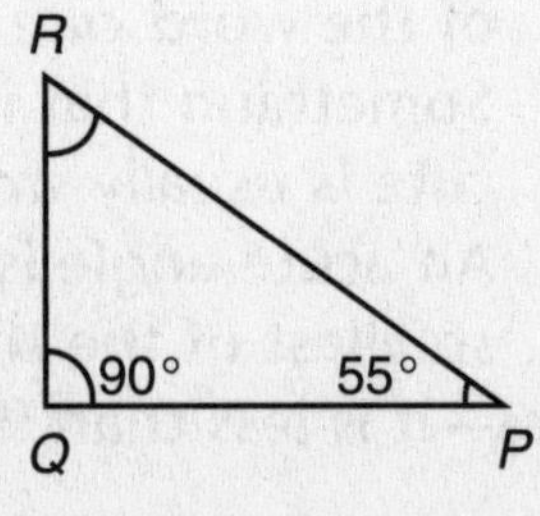

∠R: ________

Directions: Read each question carefully. Fill in the bubble next to your answer choice for each question.

1 Tamika measured two angles in a triangle with a protractor. The first angle measured 68°. The second angle measured 80°. What is the measurement of the third angle?

○ **A** 22°

○ **B** 32°

○ **C** 100°

○ **D** 122°

2 One of these sets of angle measures could be the angle measures of a right triangle. Which set is it?

○ **F** 40°, 45°, 95°

○ **G** 72°, 18°, 90°

○ **H** 48°, 67°, 65°

○ **J** 80°, 60°, 40°

3 Which set of angle measures could *not* be the measures of three angles of a triangle?

○ **A** 30°, 60°, 90°

○ **B** 45°, 55°, 80°

○ **C** 80°, 85°, 15°

○ **D** 70°, 90°, 10°

4 Which of the following statements about triangles is *false*?

○ **F** In all triangles the sum of the three angles is 180°.

○ **G** It is possible for a triangle to have two right angles.

○ **H** It is possible for a triangle to have more than one acute angle.

○ **J** It is possible for a triangle to have three equal angles.

You don't always need a protractor to find the measurement of an angle in a triangle. If you are only missing the measurement of one angle in a triangle, it's easy to figure it out. You can just use the rules on page 60.

MILE 26: COORDINATE POINTS

Points on a **coordinate grid** are named after their location, which is described with two numbers. The first number tells you how far to the right of the starting point the point is located. The second number tells you how far above the starting point the point is located. The grid below shows the point (2, 5). Note: The starting point is called the **origin.** It's point (0, 0).

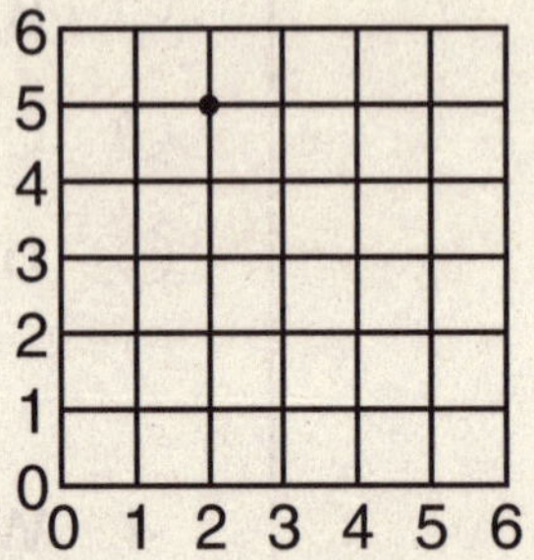

Directions: Each coordinate point below matches a letter. The blanks below list one coordinate point. Find each coordinate point and then fill in the corresponding letter in the blank. The solution spells out the answer to the riddle.

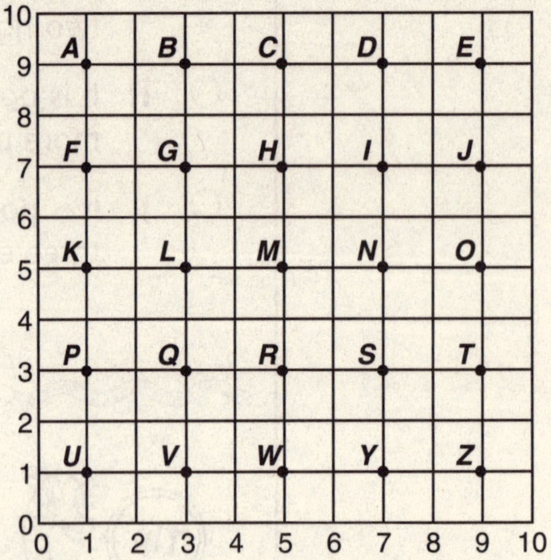

▶ **Who is bigger, Mrs. Bigger or Mrs. Bigger's baby?**

(5, 5) (5, 3) (7, 3) . (3, 9) (7, 7) (3, 7) (3, 7) (9, 9) (5, 3) , (7, 3)

(3, 9) (1, 9) (3, 9) (7, 1) (7, 7) (7, 3) (1, 9)

(3, 5) (7, 7) (9, 3) (9, 3) (3, 5) (9, 9) (3, 9) (7, 7) (3, 7) (3, 7) (9, 9) (5, 3)

Directions: Read each question carefully. Fill in the bubble next to your answer choice for each question.

1

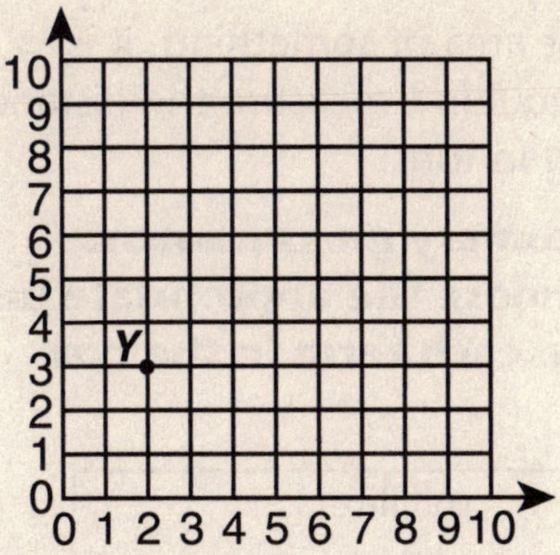

The coordinates of point *Y* are —

- ◯ **A** (2, 1)
- ◯ **B** (3, 2)
- ◯ **C** (2, 3)
- ◯ **D** (3, 3)

2

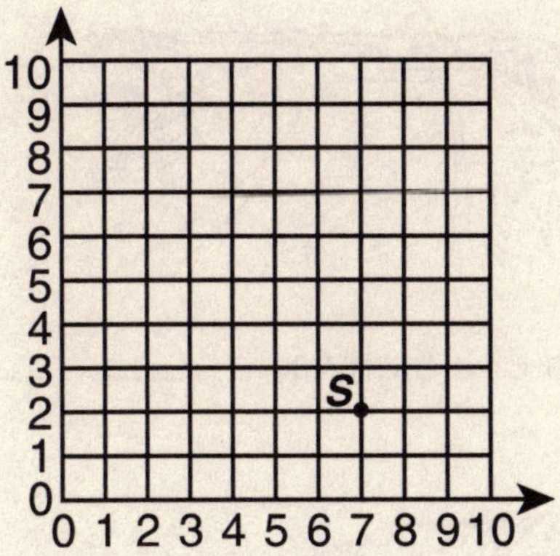

The coordinates of point *S* are —

- ◯ **F** (7, 2)
- ◯ **G** (2, 7)
- ◯ **H** (2, 2)
- ◯ **J** (7, 7)

3

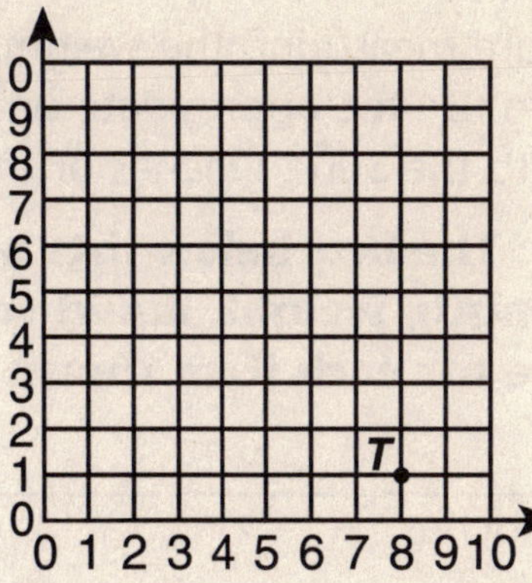

The coordinates of point *T* are —

- ◯ **A** (1, 8)
- ◯ **B** (1, 7)
- ◯ **C** (8, 1)
- ◯ **D** (7, 1)

Remember that the first number in an ordered pair tells you how far to the right a point is located. The second number in an ordered pair tells you how far up the point is located. Reversing the two numbers is a common mistake that you should try to avoid.

Mile 27: Measurement

When you are measuring the weight, distance, volume, or area of something, it is important to use the appropriate **unit of measure.** You wouldn't measure the distance from Earth to the Sun in inches or the weight of your dog in tons!

Directions: The box below lists metric and U.S. customary measurement units of length, weight, liquid volume, and area. Choose the appropriate unit of measure for each item shown below. You will use each term in the box only once.

inches	grams	milliliters
meters	tons	gallons
miles		square kilometers

1\.

The weight of a truck ____________

2\.

The area of a farm ____________

3\.

The amount of liquid in a test tube ____________

4\.

The height of a basketball player ____________

5\.

The amount of water in a fish tank ____________

6\.

The length of a highway ____________

7\.

The weight of a feather ____________

8\.

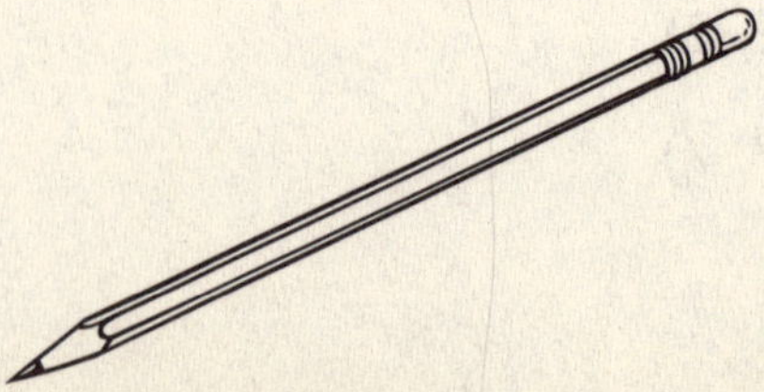

The length of a pencil ____________

Directions: Read each question carefully. Fill in the bubble next to your answer choice for each question.

1

Marny caught a big fish. Which unit would be best to measure the weight of the fish?

- ○ **A** Gallons
- ○ **B** Tons
- ○ **C** Feet
- ○ **D** Pounds

2 **Which measuring device would be most helpful to someone who wanted to figure out the length of a tennis court?**

- ○ **F** A measuring cup
- ○ **G** A yardstick
- ○ **H** A doctor's scale
- ○ **J** A 1-gallon bucket

3

The children ran a race from one tree to another. The distance between the two trees should probably be measured in —

- ○ **A** kilometers
- ○ **B** millimeters
- ○ **C** liters
- ○ **D** meters

Some questions will ask you to pick the appropriate unit of measure for a problem. Some answer choices will be the wrong type of measurements. For example, the problem may ask about measuring weight, and some answer choices may name measures of distance. Get rid of these choices right away!

Mile 28: Length

Whether you are using the metric system or the U.S. customary system, measuring distance is a great way to figure out how far you've gone and how far you're going.

Metric System	Customary System
10 millimeters (mm) = 1 centimeter (cm)	12 inches (in.) = 1 foot (ft.)
100 centimeters (cm) = 1 meter (m)	3 feet = 1 yard (yd.)
1,000 meters (m) = 1 kilometer (km)	5,280 feet = 1 mile (mi.)

Use these approximate values to compare metric and customary distances.

1 inch is about 2.5 centimeters.

1 yard is about 0.9 meters.

1 mile is about 1.5 kilometers.

Directions: Solve the problems below. Your solutions will create a code. Use the code to fill in the blanks at the bottom of the page to find the answer to the riddle.

1. 36 inches = B feet B = ____________
2. 1.5 meters = H centimeters H = ____________
3. 5 yards = E feet E = ____________
4. 7 centimeters = U millimeters U = ____________
5. 10,560 feet = D miles D = ____________
6. 0.5 kilometers = Y meters Y = ____________
7. 8 feet = A inches A = ____________
8. 80 millimeters = T centimeters T = ____________
9. 246 feet = C yards C = ____________
10. 32 centimeters = L millimeters L = ____________

► The vegetables had a race. Which vegetable won?

320	15	8	8	70	82	15

,

3	500

96

150	15	96	2

Directions: Read each question carefully. Fill in the bubble next to your answer choice for each question.

1 Alan lives 2 miles from the movie theater. About how many kilometers does he live from the movie theater?

○ A 0.5 kilometers

○ B 1 kilometer

○ C 3 kilometers

○ D 10 kilometers

2 Alicia can throw a baseball 22 meters. About how many yards can she throw a baseball?

○ F 24 yards

○ G 30 yards

○ H 44 yards

○ J 50 yards

3 Mr. Anderson's ring finger is 10 centimeters long. About how many inches long is Mr. Anderson's ring finger?

○ A 1 inch

○ B 2.5 inches

○ C 4 inches

○ D 10 inches

4 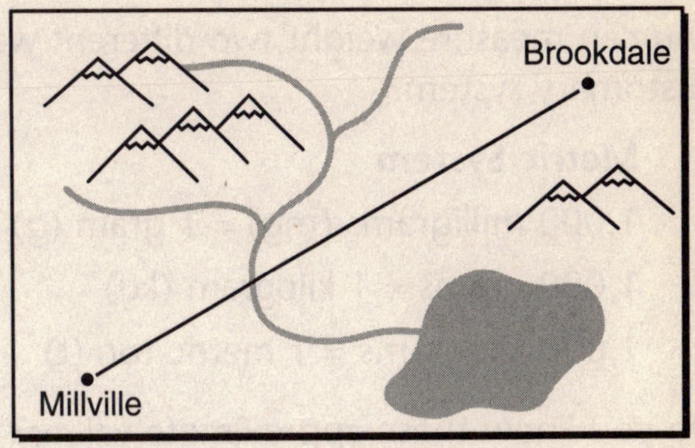

Use your centimeter ruler to answer this question.

What is the distance on the map from Millville to Brookdale?

○ F 1 centimeter

○ G 6 centimeters

○ H 15 centimeters

○ J 60 centimeters

You do not need to know exactly how many kilometers are in a mile or exactly how many inches are in a meter. You only need to know about how many. If you can make a good ballpark guess, you know all you need to know for the Virginia SOL math tests.

MILE 29: WEIGHT

You can measure weight two different ways. You can use the metric system or the U.S. customary system.

Metric System

1,000 milligrams (mg) = 1 gram (g)

1,000 grams = 1 kilogram (kg)

1,000 kilograms = 1 metric ton (t)

Customary System

16 ounces (oz.) = 1 pound (lb.)

2,000 pounds = 1 ton (T)

Do you know these approximate values? They will help you compare metric and customary weights.

1 ounce is equal to about 28 grams.
1 kilogram is a little more than 2 pounds (approximately 2.2).

Directions: Each item in the left column weighs the same as an item in the right column. Draw a line matching the two items that weigh the same.

Weight = 64 ounces

Weight = 12 pounds

Weight = 1 ton

Weight = 4,000 kilograms

Weight = 2,000 pounds

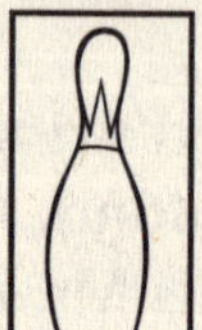

Weight = 4 pounds

Weight = 4 metric tons

Weight = 192 ounces

Directions: Read each question carefully. Fill in the bubble next to your answer choice for each question.

1

About how much does a full-grown gorilla weigh?

- ○ **A** 2 grams
- ○ **B** 20 kilograms
- ○ **C** 200 kilograms
- ○ **D** 2 metric tons

2

A knapsack full of books most likely weighs about —

- ○ **F** 10 grams
- ○ **G** 1 ounce
- ○ **H** 8 ounces
- ○ **J** 15 pounds

3 Vince bought 1 pound of apples. About how many kilograms of apples did he buy?

- ○ **A** 0.5 kilograms
- ○ **B** 5 kilograms
- ○ **C** 15 kilograms
- ○ **D** 40 kilograms

4 April weighs 80 pounds. About how many kilograms does she weigh?

- ○ **F** 20 kilograms
- ○ **G** 36 kilograms
- ○ **H** 55 kilograms
- ○ **J** 78 kilograms

A kilogram is a larger unit than a pound. The weight of an object in pounds will always be a larger number than the weight of the same object in kilograms.

MILE 30: LIQUID VOLUME

You can measure the amount of liquid in a container using the U.S. customary system or the metric system.

Metric System

1,000 milliliters (mL) = 1 liter (l)

1,000 liters = 1 kiloliter (kL)

Customary System

8 fluid ounces (fl. oz.) = 1 cup (c.)

2 cups = 16 fluid ounces = 1 pint (pt.)

2 pints = 32 fluid ounces = 1 quart (qt.)

4 quarts = 128 fluid ounces = 1 gallon (gal.)

Do you know about how many liters are in a gallon? These approximate values will help you compare measurements recorded in the U.S. customary system and the metric system.

1 liter is a little more than 1 quart.

1 gallon is a little less than 4 liters.

Directions: Solve the problems below. Write your answers in the spaces provided. Each answer has one circled space. When you have completed the exercise, the letters in the circled spaces will tell you the answer to this riddle.

► **What did the duck put in her soup?**

1. 64 fluid ounces = 2 (◯) ___ ___ ___ ___ ___ ___
2. 3 pints = 48 fluid ___ (◯) ___ ___ ___ ___
3. 14 quarts = 3.5 ___ (◯) ___ ___ ___ ___ ___
4. 1 pint = 2 (◯) ___ ___ ___
5. 4,000 liters = 4 (◯) ___ ___ ___ ___ ___ ___ ___ ___ ___
6. 2,500 milliliters = 2.5 ___ ___ ___ (◯) ___ ___
7. 3.75 liters = 3,750 ___ ___ ___ ___ ___ ___ ___ ___ (◯) ___ ___
8. 3 quarts = 6 ___ ___ ___ ___ (◯)

Directions: Read each question carefully. Fill in the bubble next to your answer choice for each question.

1 **Bonita bought 1 liter of milk. About how many quarts of milk is that?**

○ **A** 1 quart

○ **B** 4 quarts

○ **C** 8 quarts

○ **D** 12 quarts

2 **Carl bought 10 gallons of gasoline. About how many liters of gasoline did he buy?**

○ **F** 30 liters

○ **G** 40 liters

○ **H** 45 liters

○ **J** 50 liters

3 **How many ounces are in a quart?**

○ **A** 8 ounces

○ **B** 16 ounces

○ **C** 24 ounces

○ **D** 32 ounces

4 **8 pints equal —**

○ **F** 1 cup

○ **G** 1 quart

○ **H** 1 gallon

○ **J** 1 liter

5

The fish tank in the picture probably holds about how much water?

○ **A** 10 ounces

○ **B** 25 milliliters

○ **C** 10 gallons

○ **D** 2,000 gallons

A liter is about the same amount of liquid as a quart. Remembering this will help you compare all metric liquid measures with all U.S. customary liquid measures.

MILE 31: TEMPERATURE

In the United States many people use the Fahrenheit (F) scale to measure temperature. In most of the world, the Celsius (C) scale is used. Here's how the two systems compare.

Celsius	Fahrenheit
Water freezes at 0°C.	Water freezes at 32°F.
Your body temperature is usually around 37°C.	Your body temperature is usually around 98.6°F.
Water boils at 100°C.	Water boils at 212°F.

Directions: Match the temperatures in the left column with the temperatures that most nearly equal them in the right column. If the temperature in the left column is measured in degrees Celsius, match it with a temperature measured in degrees Fahrenheit in the right column. If the temperature in the left column is measured in degrees Fahrenheit, match it with a temperature measured in degrees Celsius in the right column.

1. ____

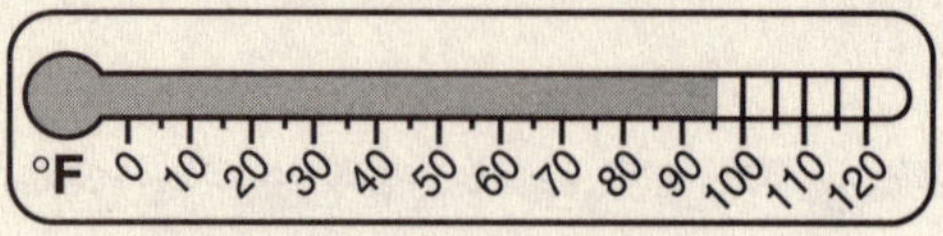

Hot Summer Day

A)

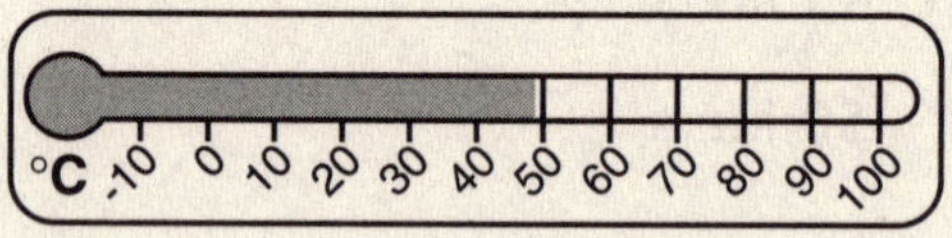

2. ____

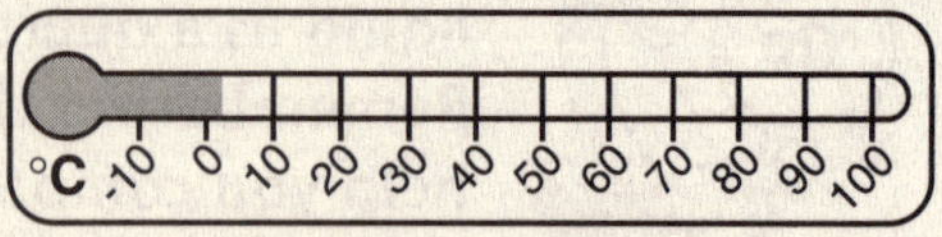

Cold Winter Day

B)

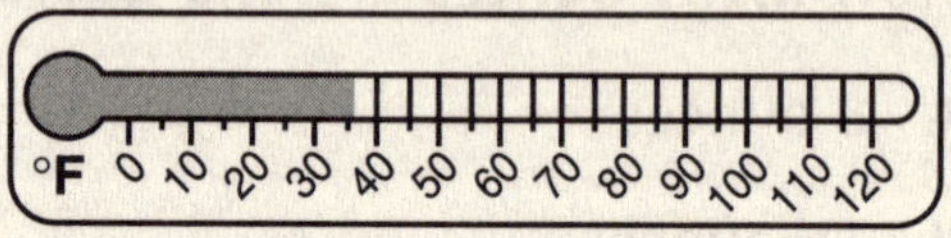

3. ____

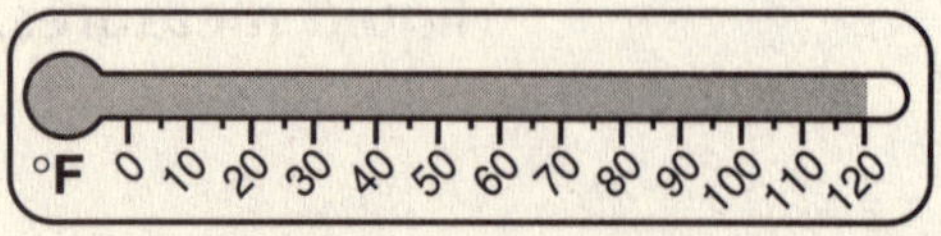

Hot Day in the Desert

C)

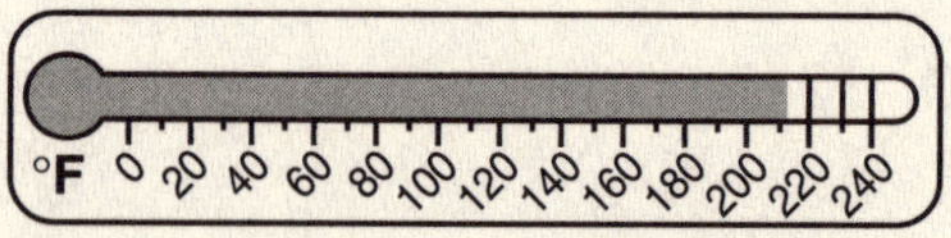

4. ____

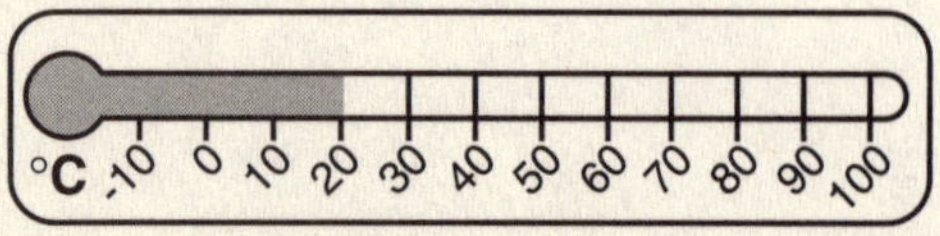

Mild Spring Day

D)

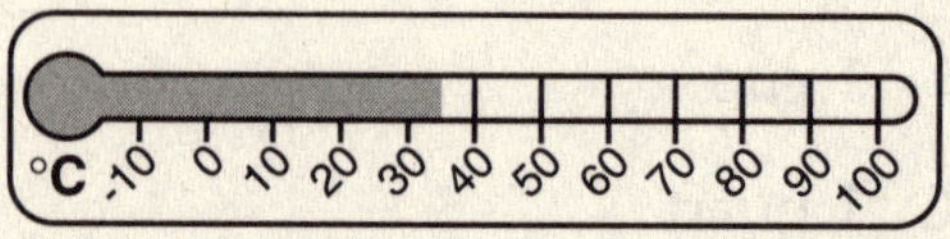

5. ____

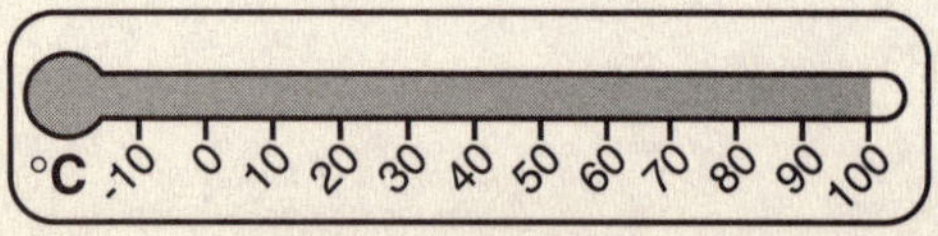

Boiling Water

E)

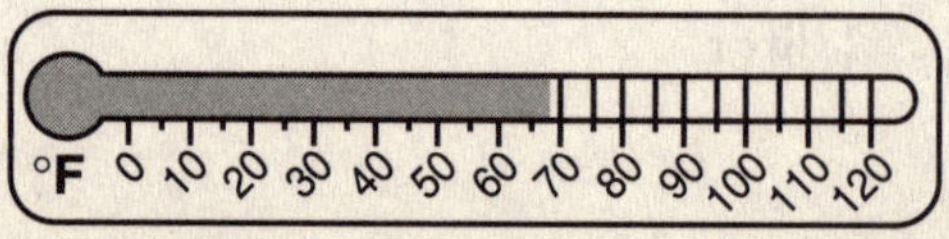

Directions: Read each question carefully. Fill in the bubble next to your answer choice for each question.

1

Wendy took her temperature. The reading on the thermometer was *most likely* —

- ○ A 32°F
- ○ B 37°F
- ○ C 99°F
- ○ D 212°F

2

Marcel took his temperature. The reading on the thermometer was *most likely* —

- ○ F 0°C
- ○ G 37°C
- ○ H 98°C
- ○ J 100°C

3 If Jackie and her father are ice fishing outdoors, which of these is the *best* estimate of the temperature?

- ○ A 28°F
- ○ B 36°F
- ○ C 20°C
- ○ D 40°C

4

In July the temperature of the ocean is about 78°F. What is the approximate temperature in degrees Celsius?

- ○ F 25°C
- ○ G 40°C
- ○ H 60°C
- ○ J 150°C

When you measure equal positive temperatures in degrees Fahrenheit and degrees Celsius, the temperature in degrees Fahrenheit will always be the greater number.

Mile 32: Time

Be careful when you figure out how much time has passed between one time and another. You cannot just add and subtract times the way you would whole numbers. That is because there are 60 minutes in an hour. Suppose you want to find out how much time passed between 2:30 P.M. and 3:25 P.M. You cannot just subtract 230 from 325. Instead, you have to imagine a clock and then count the hours and minutes between the two times.

If you do this correctly, you will discover that there are 55 minutes between 2:30 P.M. and 3:25 P.M.

Directions: Calculate the amount of time that passes between the starting time and ending time listed in each row of the table below. Look at the figure in the third column marked "Time Passed?" If the figure is correct, leave the row as is. If the figure is incorrect, cross out the entire row, including the letter in the fourth column. When you are done, the remaining letters in the fourth column will spell out the answer to the riddle. (Hint: Check out the tip on page 75 before you complete this activity.)

► **Question: What did the lawyer wear to court? Answer:** A ____________

Starting Time	Ending Time	Time Passed?	Letter
9:55 A.M.	1:10 P.M.	2 hours, 25 minutes	B
11:26 A.M.	3:15 P.M.	3 hours, 49 minutes	L
2:30 P.M.	8:04 P.M.	5 hours, 34 minutes	A
3:00 P.M.	7:49 P.M.	3 hours, 49 minutes	C
7:55 A.M.	12:48 P.M.	4 hours, 53 minutes	W
8:32 A.M.	2:04 P.M.	8 hours, 32 minutes	K
7:20 A.M.	7:10 P.M.	11 hours, 50 minutes	S
11:48 A.M.	12:10 P.M.	0 hours, 22 minutes	U
6:50 A.M.	9:10 A.M.	3 hours, 20 minutes	N
5:45 A.M.	9:19 P.M.	15 hours, 34 minutes	I
7:45 P.M.	8:15 P.M.	0 hours, 45 minutes	D
10:16 A.M.	11:51 A.M.	1 hour, 35 minutes	T

Directions: Read each question carefully. Fill in the bubble next to your answer choice for each question.

1 A play began at 7:20 P.M. The play ended at 9:04 P.M. How long did the play last?

- ○ **A** 1 hour, 24 minutes
- ○ **B** 1 hour, 44 minutes
- ○ **C** 2 hours, 16 minutes
- ○ **D** 2 hours, 24 minutes

2 Ms. Henderson started taking a walk at 9:06 A.M. She finished her walk at 11:38 A.M. How long did her walk last?

- ○ **F** 1 hour, 32 minutes
- ○ **G** 1 hour, 44 minutes
- ○ **H** 2 hours, 28 minutes
- ○ **J** 2 hours, 32 minutes

3 Michael left his house on his bicycle at 3:28 P.M. He passed the library at 4:01 P.M. How long did it take Michael to ride his bicycle from his house to the library?

- ○ **A** 23 minutes
- ○ **B** 27 minutes
- ○ **C** 32 minutes
- ○ **D** 33 minutes

4 A school cafeteria began serving lunch at 11:13 A.M. It finished serving lunch at 2:09 P.M. How long did the school cafeteria serve lunch?

- ○ **F** 1 hour, 47 minutes
- ○ **G** 2 hours, 47 minutes
- ○ **H** 2 hours, 56 minutes
- ○ **J** 3 hours, 4 minutes

5 Lindsay began reading a book at 8:37 A.M. She stopped reading at 2:56 P.M. How long did Lindsay read?

- ○ **A** 6 hours, 19 minutes
- ○ **B** 7 hours, 33 minutes
- ○ **C** 10 hours, 19 minutes
- ○ **D** 11 hours, 33 minutes

Here's an example of how to calculate elapsed time: How much time passes between 10:55 A.M. and 1:24 P.M.? First, count all the complete hours: 11 A.M. to 12 P.M., 12 P.M. to 1 P.M. There are 2 complete hours. Next, count the number of minutes from 10:55 A.M. until the end of the hour (11:00 A.M.). There are 5 minutes. Next, count the number of minutes from 1:00 P.M. to 1:24 P.M. There are 24 minutes. Add 5 and 24 to get 29 minutes. The answer to the question is 2 hours and 29 minutes.

Follow these steps for each problem that asks for the elapsed time.

Mile 33: Bar Graphs

Directions: Answer the following questions. Match the answers with a letter in the code box below. The matching letters in the code box will complete the answer to the riddle at the bottom of the page. The answer to question 1 will match up with the first missing letter in the answer, and so on.

1.

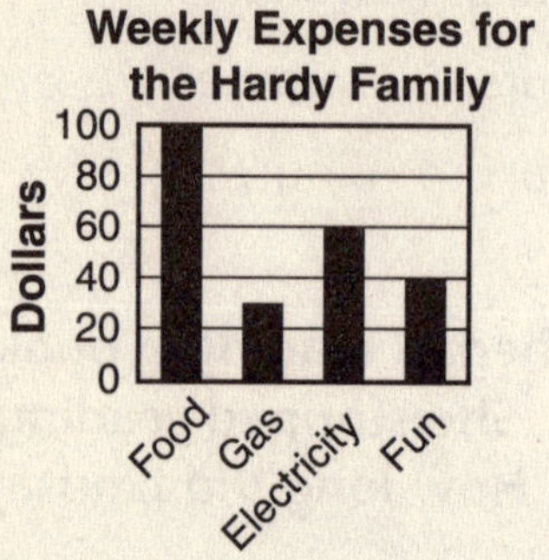

How many dollars does the Hardy family spend on gas each week?

____

2.

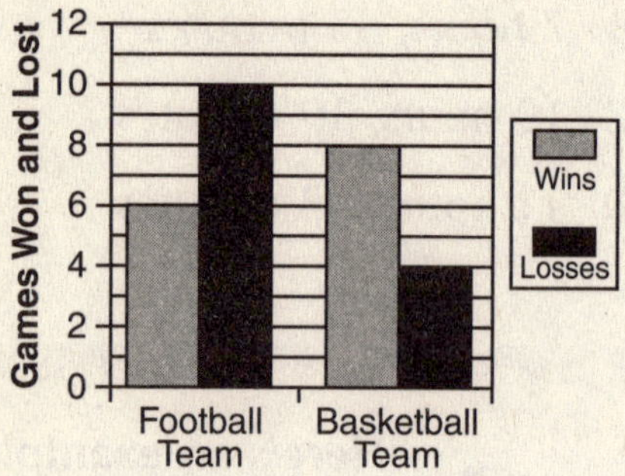

Fillmore High School has a football team and a basketball team. According to the graph, how many more games did the basketball team win than the football team? ________

3.

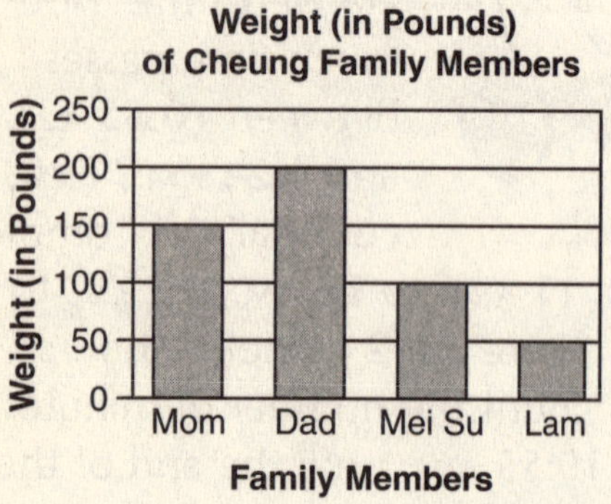

The graph shows the weights of the four members of the Cheung family. Dad weighs how many more pounds than Mei Su? ________

Code Box

16	100	60	2	5	30	92	3
A	**O**	**T**	**S**	**C**	**M**	**U**	**I**

▶ If athletes get athlete's foot, what do astronauts get?

__I__SILE T__E

Directions: Read each question carefully. Fill in the bubble next to your answer choice for each question.

1 The Riverdale High School football team did very well this year. They won more games than they lost.

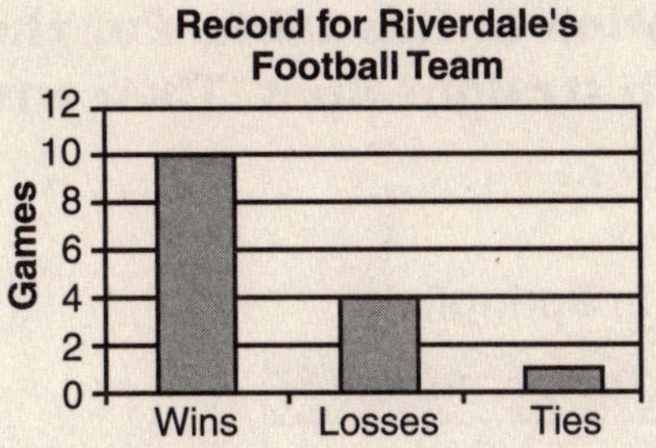

How many games did Riverdale play this year?

- ○ A 1
- ○ B 4
- ○ C 10
- ○ D 15

2 This graph shows the number of houses on eight different streets in the town of Glenville.

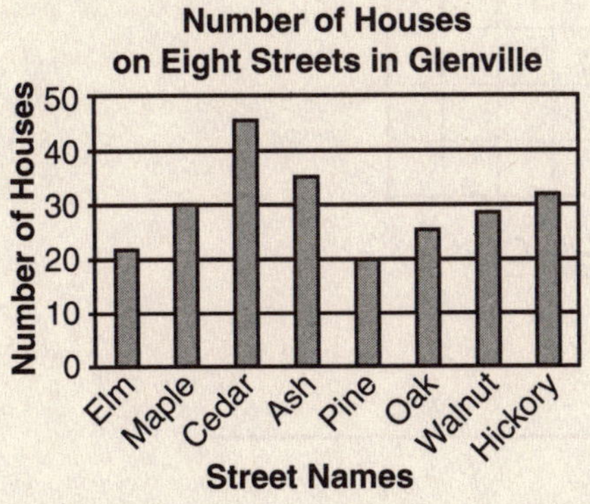

Which answer is closest to the number of houses on Oak Street?

- ○ F 21
- ○ G 25
- ○ H 30
- ○ J 32

3 What type of graph is shown here?

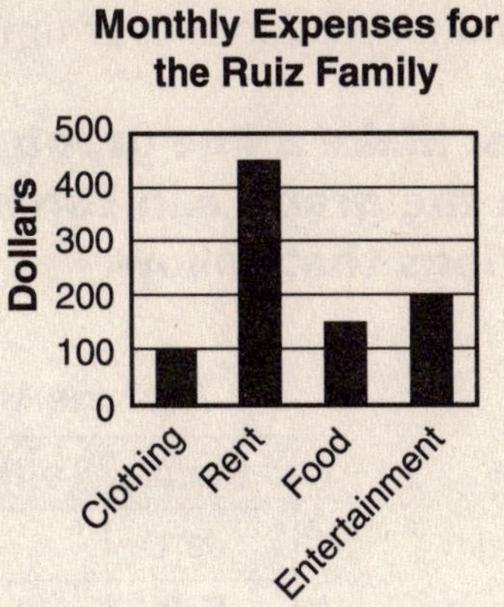

- ○ A Bar graph
- ○ B Pie chart
- ○ C Scatterplot
- ○ D Picture graph

4 Based on the information in the above graph, how much does the Ruiz family spend on clothing each *year*?

- ○ F $100
- ○ G $450
- ○ H $1,000
- ○ J $1,200

Take your time and read graphs carefully before answering the questions. Read all of the labels on each graph so that you know what information is contained in the graph.

Mile 34: Line Graphs

A **line graph** connects data points together with a straight line. That way you can see how information changes over time.

Directions: Make a line graph using the information in this table. Put the points on the graph and connect the points with straight lines. Then answer the questions that follow.

Average Monthly Temperatures in Springfield

Month	Temperature (°F)	Month	Temperature (°F)
Jan.	30°	July	85°
Feb.	25°	Aug.	75°
March	38°	Sept.	68°
April	50°	Oct.	55°
May	65°	Nov.	35°
June	75°	Dec.	30°

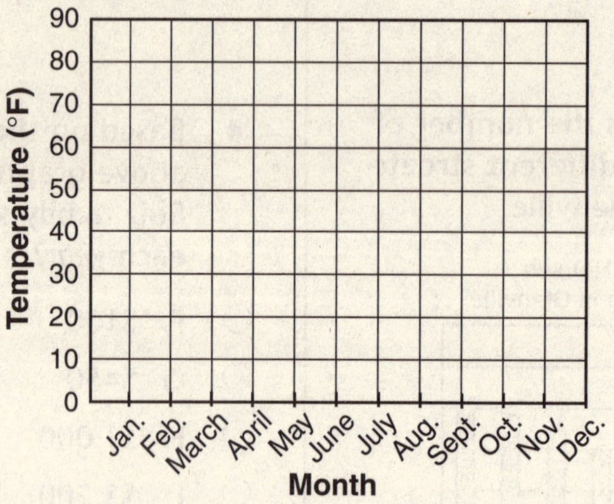

1. What is the hottest month of the year? ______________________

   The coldest? ______________________

2. Between which two months is there the *greatest increase* in average temperature?

   ____

3. Between which two months is there the *greatest decrease* in average temperature?

   ____

Directions: Read each question carefully. Fill in the bubble next to your answer choice for each question.

1 Mr. Brown's science class collected information about the growth of a bean sprout. The class measured the height of the plant each week and recorded the data in a notebook. After four weeks the class had the following data and decided to graph it.

Week	Height (inches)
1	0.5
2	1.0
3	2.0
4	3.5

Which graph correctly shows the information above?

○ A
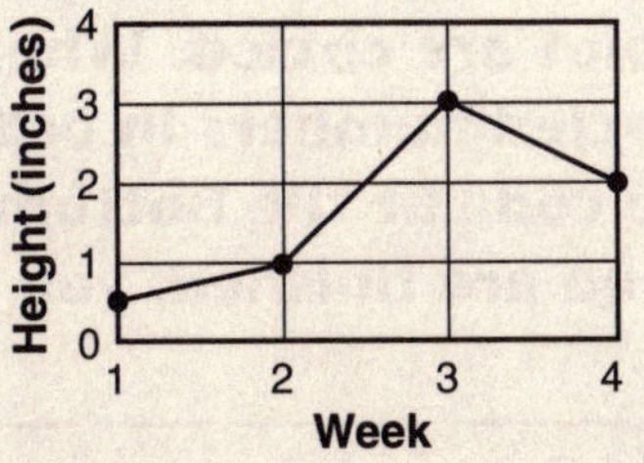

○ B
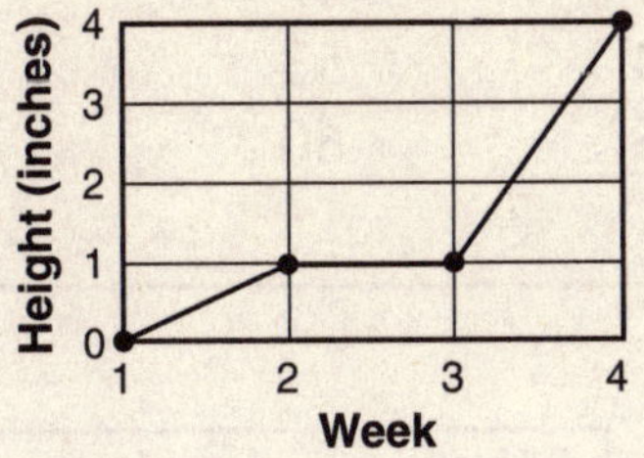

○ C
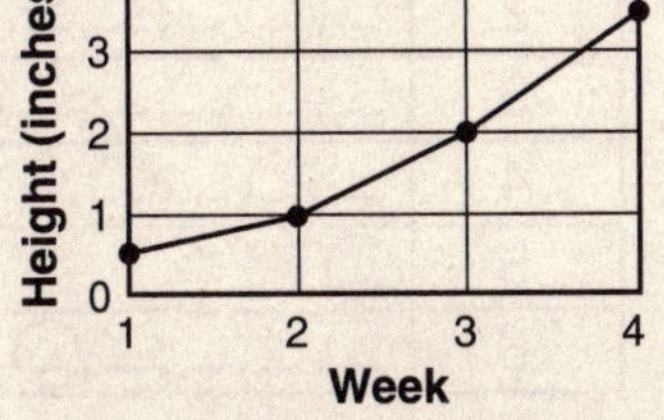

○ D
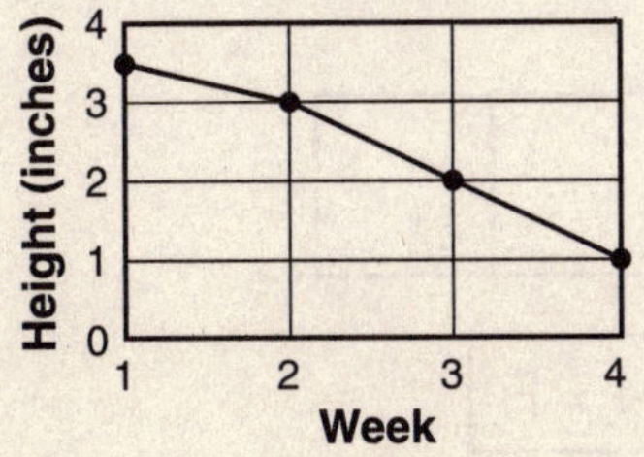

2 Jill kept a record of how many laps she ran around the school track. She did this for 6 days. She ran 4 laps on the first day, 3 on the second, then 5 on the third, 6 on the fourth, 3 on the fifth, and 7 on the sixth day. Which line graph shows this information?

○ F
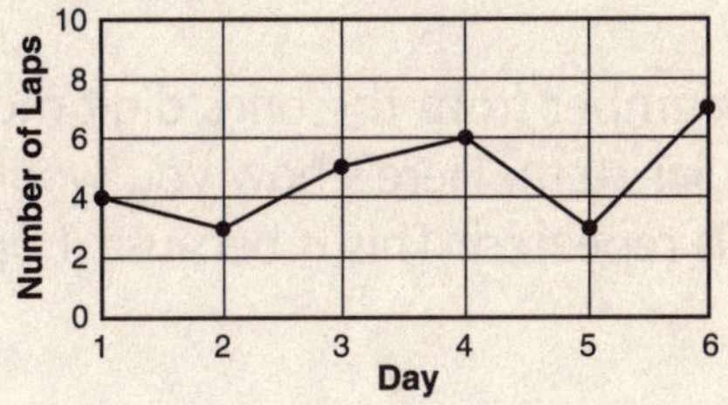

○ G
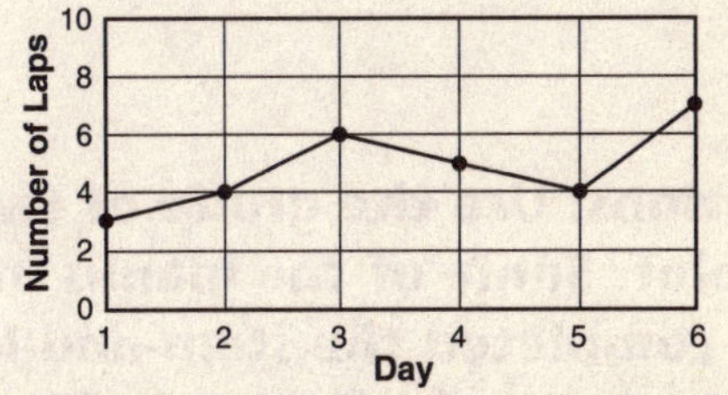

○ H
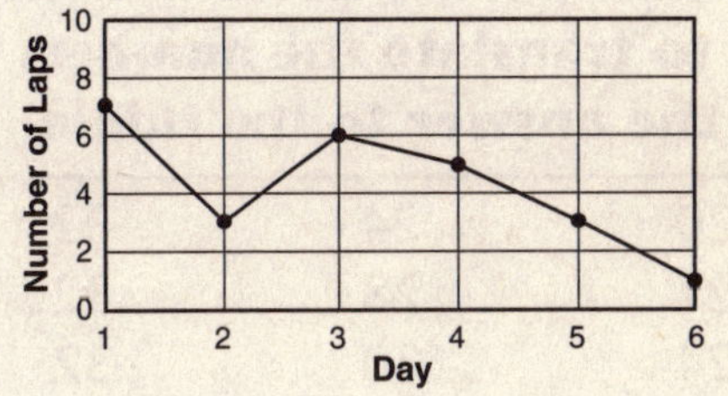

○ J
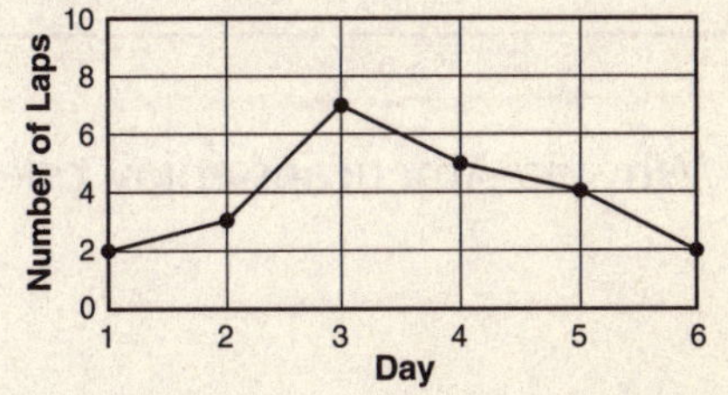

It's easy to confuse points on a graph that are close to each other. Lay a ruler or the straight edge of a piece of paper on the graph to help you line up the points with the labels on the sides of the graph.

MILE 35: STEM-AND-LEAF PLOTS

You can display data in a **stem-and-leaf plot.** Stem-and-leaf plots are great for displaying lists of two-digit numbers. List the tens digits in the left column of the plot, in order from least to greatest. List the ones digits in the leaf beside the appropriate tens digit, in order from least to greatest. Here's how you would write 45 in a stem-and-leaf plot.

Stem	Leaf
4	5

List a number from the ones digit more than once if it appears more than once with a particular stem. Here's how you would list the numbers 45, 47, 50, 51, and 51. Notice how the 1 is repeated. This is because 1 appears twice with the stem 5 in the list of numbers.

Stem	Leaf
4	5,7
5	0,1,1

Directions: Use the group of two-digit numbers below to fill in the stem-and-leaf plot. Some of the blanks in the stem-and-leaf plot are circled. When you have completed the stem-and-leaf plot, copy the circled numbers in order in the blanks at the bottom of the page. Then use the code at the bottom of the page to translate the numbers into letters. When you are finished, you will have the answer to the riddle.

20	24	32	35	41	47	61
21	28	32	36	44	53	61
24	30	32	36	45	60	65
						69

► Why do Americans enjoy celebrating Flag Day?

Stem	Leaf
2	_, (_), _, _, _
3	(_), _, _, _, _, (_), (_)
4	_, (_), _, (_)
5	(_)
6	(_), _, _, _, (_)

Because it's always a

0 = A	1 = B	2 = C	3 = D	4 = E
5 = L	6 = N	7 = R	8 = T	9 = Y

Directions: Read each question carefully. Fill in the bubble next to your answer choice for each question.

1 Cindy received these scores on the quizzes given by her science teacher.

88	88	83	80
75	86	96	98
92	98	91	76
95	79	79	87

Which stem-and-leaf plot represents the same set of data?

○ A

Stem	Leaf
7	5, 6, 9, 9
8	0, 3, 6, 7, 8, 8
9	1, 2, 5, 6, 8, 8

○ B

Stem	Leaf
7	5, 6, 9
8	3, 6, 7, 8
9	1, 2, 5, 6, 8

○ C

Stem	Leaf
7	5, 6, 9
8	0, 3, 6, 7, 8
9	1, 2, 5, 6, 8

○ D

Stem	Leaf
7	0, 5, 6, 9
8	0, 3, 6, 7, 8
9	0, 1, 2, 5, 6, 8

2 This stem-and-leaf plot shows the high temperature, in degrees Fahrenheit, in a town every day for the first two weeks of March.

Stem	Leaf
5	0, 3, 3, 6, 8, 9
6	2, 2, 2, 5
7	0, 1, 1, 4
8	

Which of the following lists all the data that appears in the stem-and-leaf plot?

○ F 50°F, 53°F, 56°F, 58°F, 59°F, 62°F, 65°F, 70°F, 71°F

○ G 50°F, 53°F, 56°F, 58°F, 59°F, 60°F, 62°F, 62°F, 65°F, 70°F, 71°F, 80°F

○ H 50°F, 53°F, 53°F, 56°F, 58°F, 59°F, 62°F, 62°F, 62°F, 65°F, 70°F, 71°F, 71°F, 74°F

○ J 50°F, 53°F, 53°F, 56°F, 58°F, 59°F, 60°F, 62°F, 62°F, 65°F, 70°F, 71°F, 71°F, 80°F

Remember that numbers can be repeated in a stem-and-leaf plot. If a set of data includes a number seven times, then that number must appear in the stem-and-leaf plot seven times. The wrong answer choices on stem-and-leaf questions often will not list some numbers enough times.

Mile 36: Data

2, 4, 6, 9, 14

The **average,** or **mean,** of the five numbers above is the sum of the numbers (2 + 4 + 6 + 9 + 14 = 35) divided by 5. The average (mean) of these numbers is 35 ÷ 5, or 7.

The **mode** is the number that appears most often in a group of numbers. Some groups don't have a mode, while other groups may have two or more modes. In the data set {2, 3, 3, 5, 7, 9} the mode is 3 because 3 is the number that appears most often.

Directions: Solve each of the following problems and write your answers in the spaces in the cross-number puzzle below. Have a calculator ready, because some of the numbers will be hard to figure out on your own.

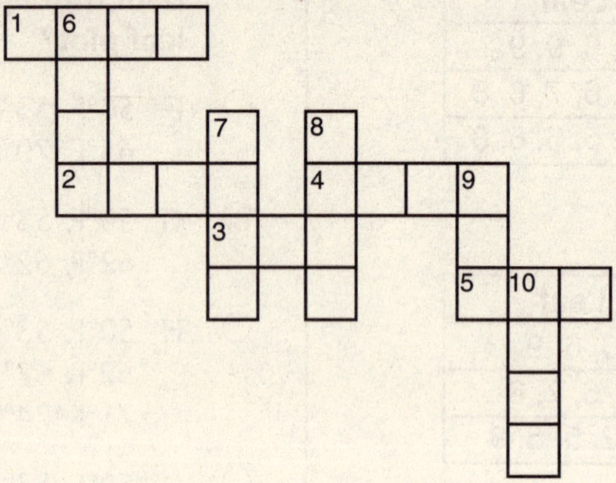

Across

1. The mean of 2,356; 1,198; 3,422; and 4,332
2. The mean of 987; 1,256; and 2,449
3. The mean of 367; 278; 101; and 398
4. The mean of 1,754; 967; 996; and 431
5. The mean of 380; 168; 215; and 117

Down

6. The mode of 6,475; 7,821; 8,231; 6,593; and 8,231
7. The mode of 3,421; 3,583; 3,421; 3,583; and 3,421
8. The mode of 5,673; 3,168; 3,168; 8,003; 5,673; and 3,168
9. The mode of 280; 280; 546; 712; 546; 712; 268; and 712
10. The mode of 1,845; 2,291; 3,769; 6,646; and 2,291

Directions: Read each question carefully. Fill in the bubble next to your answer choice for each question.

1 Look at this set of data.

17	28	19	21
21	30	21	37
37	22	26	15

What is the mode of this set of data?

○ A 19

○ B 21

○ C 28

○ D 37

2 In the last game of the season, the Oakwood High School basketball team scored 55 points. This is a list of how many points each player scored.

Player	Points
Walt	11
Zhang	14
Earle	9
Kaleel	15
Tom	6

What was the mean (average) number of points scored by each player on the team?

○ F 9

○ G 11

○ H 14

○ J 15

3 Sherry caught a firefly in a jar. She then watched the firefly for 5 hours, counting how many times the firefly lit up during each hour. This table shows her results.

5:00 P.M. to 6:00 P.M.	25 times
6:00 P.M. to 7:00 P.M.	26 times
7:00 P.M. to 8:00 P.M.	26 times
8:00 P.M. to 9:00 P.M.	22 times
9:00 P.M. to 10:00 P.M.	31 times

What was the mean (average) number of times the firefly lit up in one hour?

○ A 25 times

○ B 26 times

○ C 27 times

○ D 130 times

You don't have to do any mathematical calculations to find the mode of a set of data. The mode is easy to find. Just identify the number that appears most often in a set of data. Be sure to remember the definition of *mode* and *mean* when you take the Virginia SOL math test. If you get them mixed up, you'll probably answer many data questions incorrectly.

MILE 37: NUMBER LINES

A **number line** shows you how numbers relate to one another. Numbers on the left side of a number line are smaller than the numbers on the right side of the number line. The greater the distance between two numbers on the number line, the greater the difference in their values.

Some number lines are divided into units of one. In the number line below, each mark represents a value one greater than the value to its left.

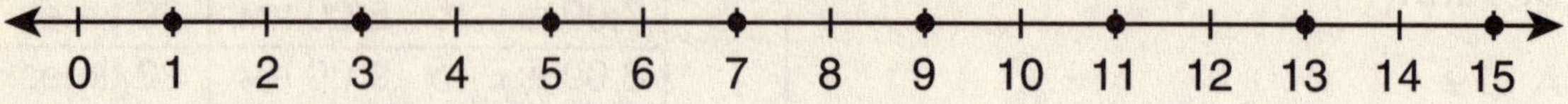

Some are divided into larger units. The number line below is divided into units of 25.

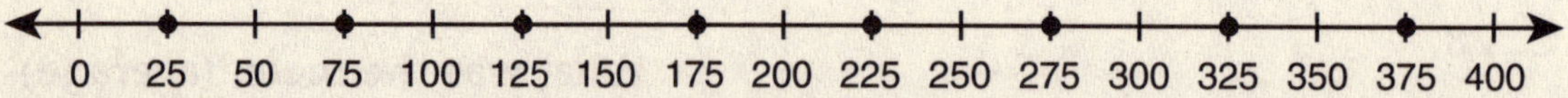

Directions: Each of the number lines below is divided into a different number of units. Figure out the number of units each mark on the number line represents. Then write the number in the blank to the right of the number line. Next to each blank is a letter. When you have filled in all the blanks, rearrange the numbers and letters next to them so that the numbers are in order from least to greatest. After you rearrange the letters correctly, you will unscramble the answer to the riddle.

1. 

______________ **(I)**

2. 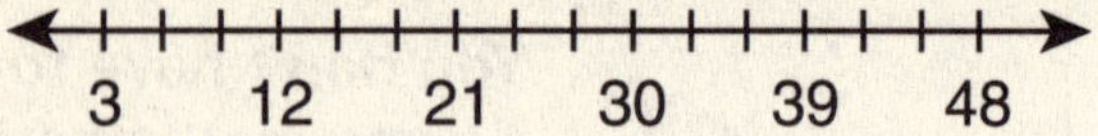

______________ **(S)**

3. 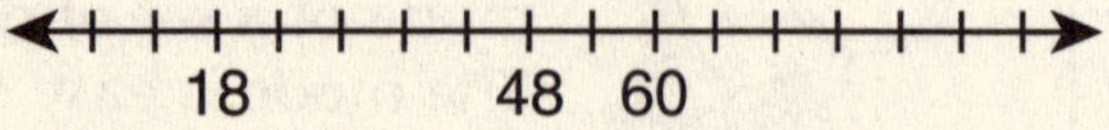

______________ **(C)**

4. 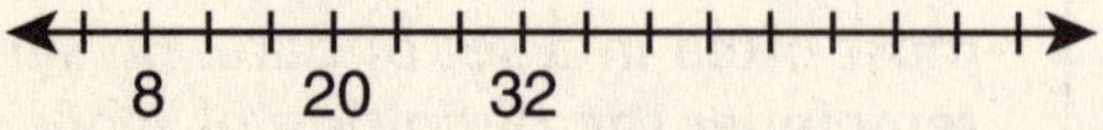

______________ **(T)**

5. 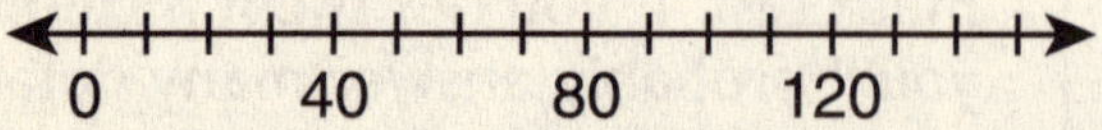

______________ **(K)**

▶ What do you call a boomerang that doesn't come back?

Answer: *A* ______________________________

Directions: Read each question carefully. Fill in the bubble next to your answer choice for each question.

1

Point *X* represents what value on the number line?

- ○ A 48
- ○ B 60
- ○ C 70
- ○ D 90

2

Point *P* represents what value on the number line?

- ○ F 8
- ○ G 9
- ○ H 10
- ○ J 12

3

Point *G* represents what value on the number line?

- ○ A 28
- ○ B 32
- ○ C 36
- ○ D 40

4

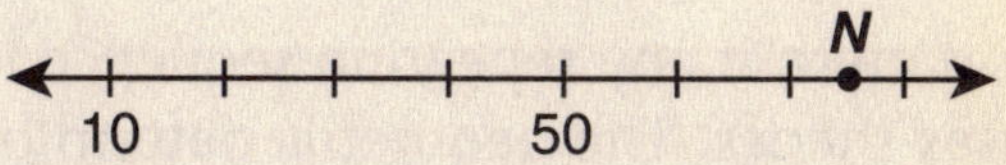

Which is closest to the value of point *N* on the number line?

- ○ F 52
- ○ G 53
- ○ H 62
- ○ J 75

When you take the Virginia SOL math test, use scratch paper to copy the number line from the test booklet. Then, fill in any missing numbers on the number line. This will help you avoid making careless mistakes.

Example:

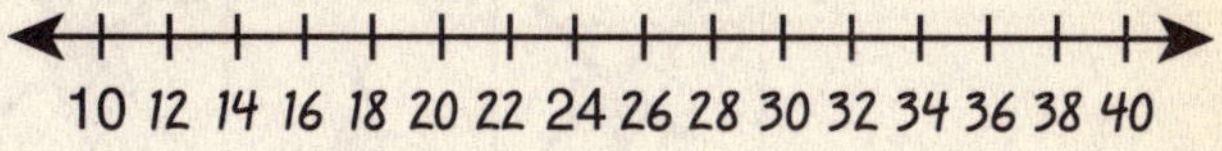

Mile 38: Geometric Patterns

A pattern is any repeating sequence that follows a set of rules. A **geometric pattern** uses shapes. The geometric pattern below follows the rule "square, triangle, star, square, triangle, star…." Once you recognize a pattern, you can guess what shape will come next. In the following pattern the next shape will be a square.

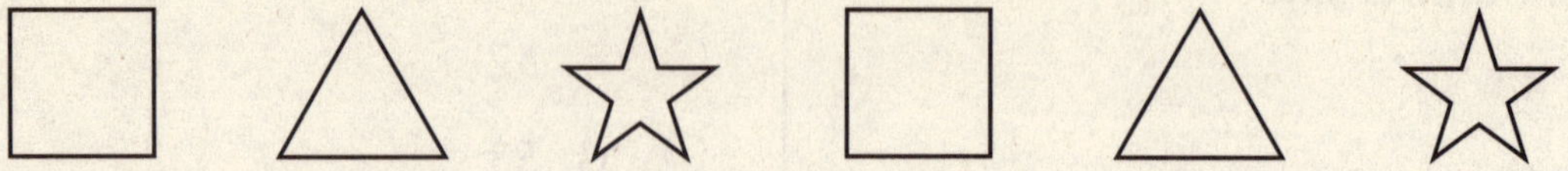

Sometimes patterns get a little more complicated. The next pattern uses the "square, triangle, star" pattern above but adds a shading pattern of "shaded, white."

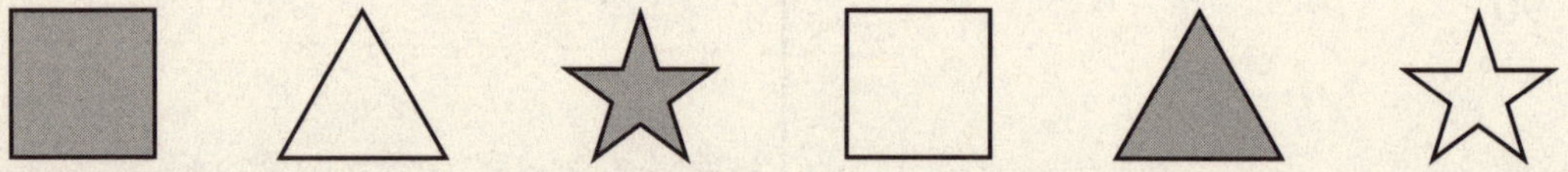

What will the next figure be in the pattern above? If you said a shaded square, you're correct!

Directions: Study the following pattern and then look at each of the shapes in the table. Some of the shapes continue the pattern; others do not. Cross out the boxes with shapes that do not continue the pattern. The letters in the boxes you do NOT cross out will spell out the name of a great Italian artist of the Renaissance. The first row has been done for you.

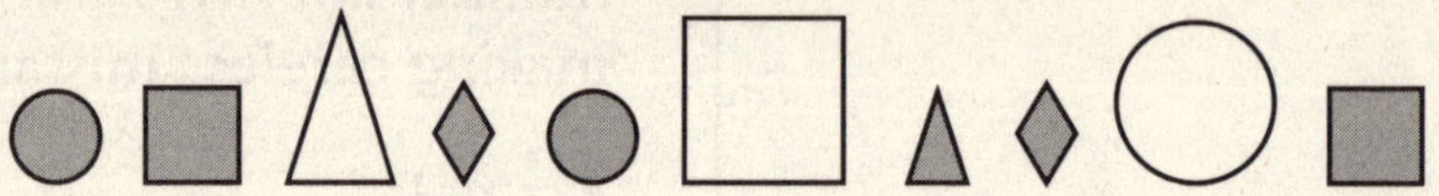

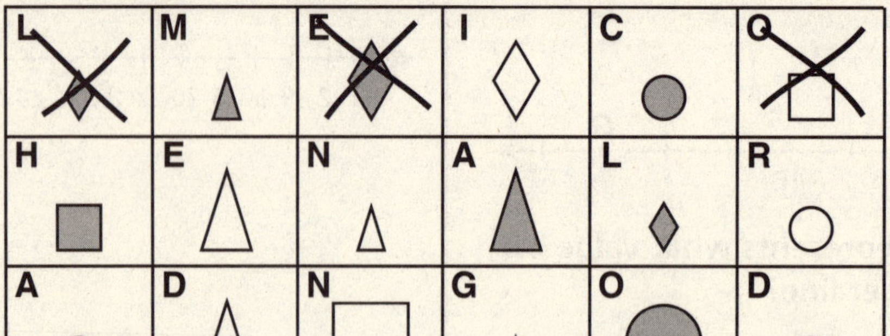

▶ **What is the name of the famous artist?**

___ ___ ___ ___ ___ ___ ___ ___ ___ ___ ___ ___

Directions: Read each question carefully. Fill in the bubble next to your answer choice for each question.

1 Study this pattern.

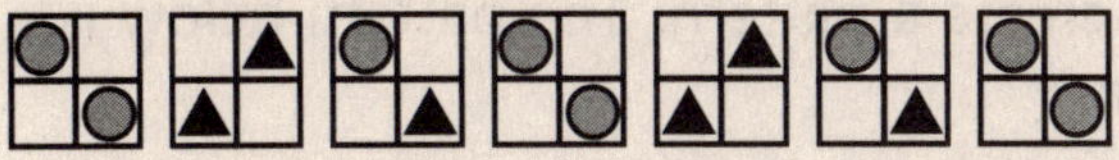

What will the *ninth* shape in the pattern look like if the pattern continues?

○ A 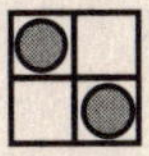

○ B 

○ C 

○ D 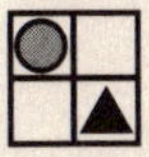

2 Study this pattern.

What will the *tenth* shape in the pattern look like if the pattern continues?

○ F 

○ G 

○ H 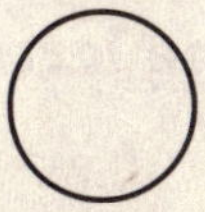

○ J 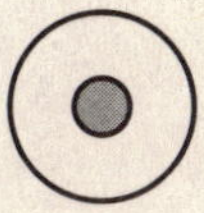

Number each type of shape in a geometric pattern. Numbering each shape makes it easier to predict what shapes will come next in the pattern. For example, if the first shape in the pattern is a gray circle, all gray circles in the pattern should be number 1. If the second shape in the pattern is a white square, then all white squares in the pattern should be number 2. Keep numbering the shapes until no new ones appear in the pattern.

Mile 39: Number Patterns

You can add, subtract, multiply, or divide to create a **number pattern.** Just perform the same operation on each number in a sequence to create a pattern. The pattern below is formed by adding 3 to each number in the pattern.

1, 4, 7, 10, 13, 16, 19, . . .

Some patterns are a little more complicated. The pattern below switches between two sets of numbers. You add 2 to the first number to get the third, and then you add 2 to the third number to get the fifth, and so on. You also add 4 to the second number to get the fourth, and then add 4 to the fourth number to get the sixth, and so on.

1, 6, 3, 10, 5, 14, 7, 18, . . .

Directions: Figure out each pattern and then fill in each blank with the number that comes next in the pattern. Each answer will match up with a number in the code at the bottom of the page. Translate each number into a letter using the code. Then copy the letters into the boxes at the bottom of the page to reveal the name of a famous American inventor. In the first box you should write the letter that goes with the number in pattern 1, and so on.

1. 2, 5, 4, 9, 6, 13, ____
2. 1, 2, 4, 8, ____
3. 2, 4, 6, 8, 10, ____
4. 11, 22, 33, ____
5. 2, 1, 5, 2, 8, 3, ____
6. 96, 48, 24, ____
7. 6, 8, 14, 18, 22, 28, ____
8. 5, 10, 15, ____
9. 1, 2, 10, 4, 12, 6, 14, ____
10. 7, 14, 21, 28, 35, 42, ____

A = 1	B = 4	C = 5	D = 7	E = 8	F = 9	G = 10	H = 11	I = 12
J = 13	K = 14	L = 16	M = 17	N = 20	O = 21	P = 22	Q = 23	R = 25
S = 27	T = 30	U = 31	V = 32	W = 44	X = 46	Y = 49	Z = 55	

Directions: Read each question carefully. Fill in the bubble next to your answer choice for each question.

1 What is the next number in the sequence below?

2, 4, 8, 16, 32, ___

○ A 64

○ B 56

○ C 48

○ D 40

2 15, 19, 24, 30, 37, ___, ___

Which correctly fills the blanks in this number pattern?

○ F 38, 39

○ G 45, 54

○ H 47, 57

○ J 44, 52

3 These numbers form a pattern.

20, 27, 34, 41, ___

What number belongs in the blank?

○ A 42

○ B 48

○ C 75

○ D 102

4 50, 42, 35, 29, ___, ___

Which correctly fill the blanks in this number pattern?

○ F 23, 17

○ G 25, 24

○ H 64, 22

○ J 24, 20

5 These numbers form a pattern.

5, 12, 8, 17, 11, 22, 14, 27, 17, 32, ___

What number belongs in the blank?

○ A 20

○ B 37

○ C 39

○ D 49

If you are confused by a number pattern, it is probably because the pattern switches between two rules. Look at every other number in the pattern and you will probably figure out the rules for the pattern pretty quickly.

MILE 40: POSSIBLE COMBINATIONS

Figuring out how many **possible combinations** there are of two or more things is like mixing and matching. Let's say that Uncle Bernie is deciding what to wear. He has two shirts and three ties to mix and match.

How many possible combinations of *one shirt* and *one tie* can Uncle Bernie choose from? You just have to count to figure it out. Each shirt can go with one of 3 different ties. So, there are 3 possible combinations for each shirt. Because there are 2 shirts, there are 6 possible combinations ($3 \times 2 = 6$). (Note: Multiplication can sometimes help you find the number of possible combinations when there are *two* things to mix and match.)

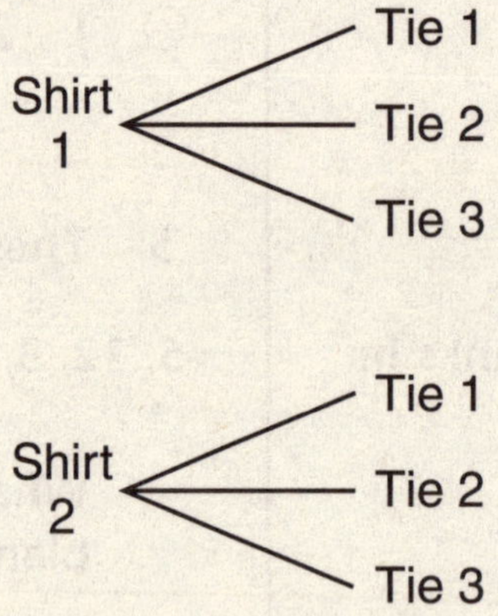

Directions: It's Saturday afternoon and you are hanging out with your friends. You are all hungry, so you decide to order a pizza. Read the short passage below and figure out how many different types of pizza you can order.

The pizzeria offers a choice of three toppings: sausage, peppers, and extra cheese. It is possible for you to order a pizza with no toppings, one topping, two toppings, or all three toppings. Before you decide, you and your friends want to figure out how many different types of pies you can order. Write the all of the different possible combinations below.

____

____

____

____

____

____

____

____

How many different pies is it possible for you to choose from? ________

Which pie would you choose? They all sound pretty good!

Directions: Read each question carefully. Fill in the bubble next to your answer choice for each question.

1 Campers at the Happy Hills Summer Camp can choose their activities for the first two periods of the day. This table shows their choices.

Period 1	Period 2
Swimming	Arts and Crafts
Music	Canoeing
Softball	

Which diagram shows all the different choices available to campers at the Happy Hills Summer Camp?

○ **A**

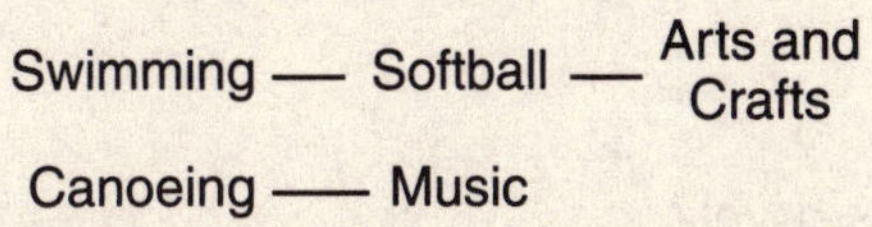

○ **B**

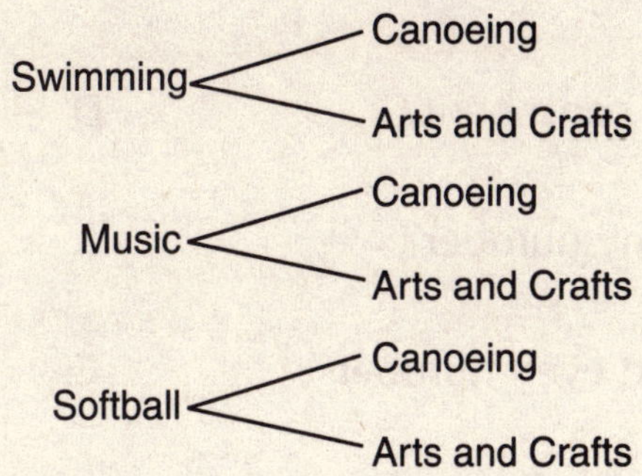

○ **C**

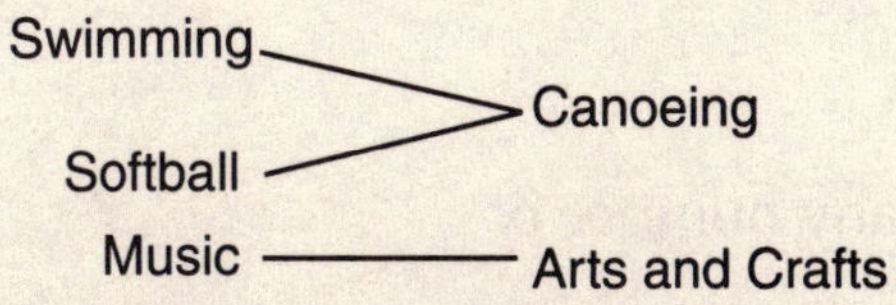

○ **D**

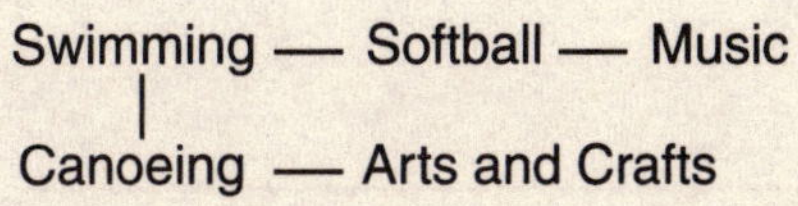

2 This tree diagram shows all the colors and sizes available for a certain style of sweater.

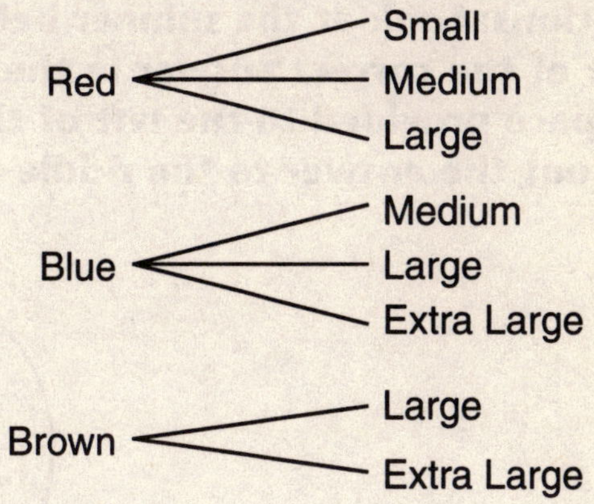

Which color sweaters are available in the Extra Large size?

○ **F** Red only

○ **G** Red and Blue only

○ **H** Blue and Brown only

○ **J** Red, Blue, and Brown

Remember that you must start a different column for each different type of item in a diagram. If you are diagramming combinations of colors and sizes, for example, you must have one column for colors and one column for sizes.

So, in question 2 above, the first column lists colors (to the left of the branches) and the second column lists sizes (to the right of the branches).

Mile 41: Probability

Probability is the chance that an event will happen. It is usually expressed as a ratio between 0 and 1.

Directions: Look at the spinner below. Read each question and find the letter of the correct answer in the column on the right. Write the letter in the space provided to the left of the question. The letters going down will spell out the answer to the riddle at the bottom of the page.

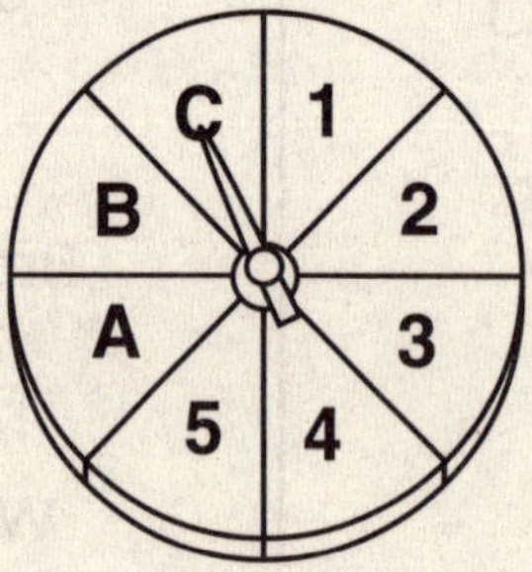

______	**1.** What is the probability of landing on a vowel?	**H**	$\frac{3}{8}$
______	**2.** What is the probability of landing on an odd number?	**E**	$\frac{2}{8}$
______	**3.** What is the probability of landing on a consonant?	**D**	$\frac{7}{8}$
______	**4.** What is the probability of landing on any number?	**S**	$\frac{4}{8}$
______	**5.** What is the probability of landing on an even number *or* a consonant?	**C**	$\frac{1}{8}$
______	**6.** What is the probability of landing on any number *or* a consonant?	**W**	$\frac{5}{8}$
______	**7.** What is the probability of landing on any number *or* any letter?	**Y**	$\frac{6}{8}$
______	**8.** What is the probability of landing on an odd number *or* any letter?	**A**	$\frac{8}{8}$

► On what day do monsters eat? ______________________________

Directions: Read each question carefully. Fill in the bubble next to your answer choice for each question.

1 A bag of marbles has four black marbles, five white marbles, and one gray marble.

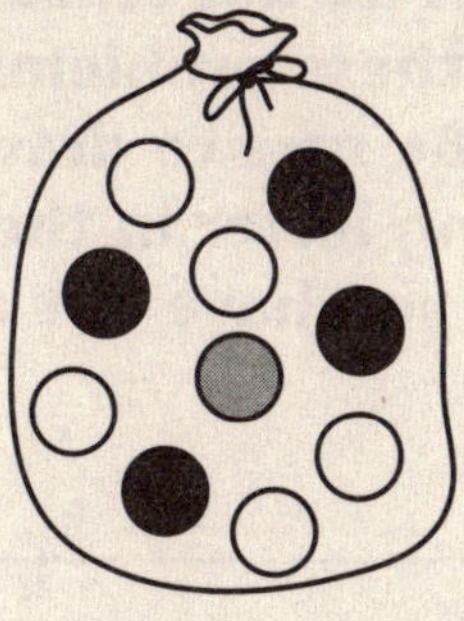

Howard reached into the bag and chose one marble without looking. What is the probability that Howard pulled out a black marble?

○ **A** $\frac{9}{10}$

○ **B** $\frac{1}{2}$

○ **C** $\frac{2}{5}$

○ **D** $\frac{1}{10}$

2 Brian wrote the numbers 1 through 9 on seven index cards.

Brian turns the cards face down, shuffles them, and chooses one card at random. What is the probability that Brian will choose an odd-numbered card?

○ **F** $\frac{5}{4}$

○ **G** $\frac{5}{9}$

○ **H** $\frac{1}{2}$

○ **J** $\frac{3}{9}$

The total number of possible events will be the bottom number in a probability. The top number will be the number of ways a certain event can happen.

Mile 42: Probability Problems

Probability problems deal with the likelihood that something will happen.

Directions: Read each statement below. Some state probability problems, while others do not. Draw a line through the ones that do not state probability problems. (You don't have to solve any of these problems; you just have to figure out if they ask about probability.) Be sure to draw the line all the way across the page including the corresponding letter in the right column. If you complete the drill correctly, the letters you have not crossed out will spell out the answer to the question below.

▶ What is the second largest city in Egypt? ______________________

1. How many eggs are in a dozen? **V**
2. What is the likelihood that a roll of a number cube will result in a 5? **A**
3. How many animals at the local zoo have four legs? **D**
4. What is the chance that a playing card chosen at random will be an ace? **L**
5. How likely is it that the result of a coin toss will be heads? **E**
6. If two students are absent from a class that normally contains thirty-five students, how many students are in class? **O**
7. How likely is it that a student chosen at random from a class of twenty-five students will be the tallest student in the class? **X**
8. The weather forecast says that there is a 50 percent chance of rain tomorrow. How likely is it that it will rain? **A**
9. It snowed 1.5 inches on Monday and 3.75 inches on Tuesday. How much more snow fell on Tuesday than fell on Monday? **R**
10. A bag of seven marbles contains one white marble. What is the chance that a person selecting a marble without looking will choose the white marble? **N**
11. How likely is it that the result of a coin toss will be tails? **D**
12. A spinner has six spaces of equal size. Each is a different color. One of the colors is blue. What is the chance that a spin of the spinner will land on the blue space? **R**
13. What is the product of 2.7 and 3.106? **Z**
14. A magician chooses an assistant at random from an audience that contains twenty boys and thirty girls. Is the assistant more likely to be a boy or a girl? **I**
15. What is the likelihood that a roll of a number cube will result in a 2? **A**

Directions: Read each question carefully. Fill in the bubble next to your answer choice for each question.

1 Farmer Miller has these animals on her farm.

Which question about the animals can be answered using probability?

- ○ **A** How many four-legged animals does Farmer Miller have?
- ○ **B** If Farmer Miller chose one animal to sell at random, what type of animal would most likely be sold?
- ○ **C** If Farmer Miller sold all of her pigs, how many animals would be left on her farm?
- ○ **D** Farmer Miller has how many more goats than she has cows?

2 Greta wrote numbers on index cards as shown below.

Which question about the index cards can be answered using probability?

- ○ **F** Greta added the numbers written on her nine index cards. What was the sum of the numbers?
- ○ **G** Greta gave three of the index cards to her friend Mario. How many cards did Greta have left?
- ○ **H** Greta calculated the mode of the numbers on her cards and the average (mean) of the numbers on her cards. What is the difference between the mode and the average for the numbers on the cards?
- ○ **J** After shuffling the cards, Greta dropped them on the floor. When they landed, only one card was facing up. What number was most likely on the card?

The test may ask you to find a question that can be solved using probability. Look for a question that includes *the word likely, likelihood, probably,* or *probable.*

MILE 43: VARIABLES

So far you have used numbers to solve problems. Sometimes symbols and letters stand for certain numbers in math problems. These symbols and letters are called **variables.** You can then solve the problem and find what number the symbol stands for. Look at the example below.

$$2 + x = 5$$

What number does *x* stand for? You have to ask yourself "What number plus 2 is equal to 5?" That's easy: 3 plus 2 is equal to 5! So *x* stands for 3.

Directions: Solve each of the following problems. Find the answers in the code box below, and then write the letter that matches it in the space to the left of the problem. The letters will spell out the name of a famous cartoon character.

______ 1. If $x = 3$ and $y = 5$, what is $(x + 1) + (2 \times y)$ equal to? ______

______ 2. Imagine that $\square = 13$ and $\Delta = 12$. What is $\square + \Delta$ equal to? ______

______ 3. What number does $\square$ stand for? $(4 \times \square) + 2 = 18$ ______

______ 4. The number of cookies Nick baked is *c*. Sherine baked 6 more cookies than Nick did. So, the number of cookies Sherine baked is $c + 6$. If $c = 12$, how many cookies did Sherine bake? ______

______ 5. During the volleyball season, the boys' team won 4 fewer games than the girls' team. If *g* equals the number of games the girls won, the number of games the boys won is $g - 4$. If the girls won 10 games, how many games did the boys win? ______

______ 6. What is *x* equal to if $21 - x = 2$? ______

______ 7. If $6 \times \Delta = 30$, what number does Δ stand for? ______

______ 8. If $x = 41$ and $y = 58$, what is $x + y$ equal to? ______

Code Box

20 **Z**	86 **T**	18 **K**	21 **B**	7 **M**	19 **P**	93 **V**	6 **Y**
5 **I**	25 **O**	55 **L**	4 **R**	33 **S**	99 **G**	61 **U**	14 **P**

Directions: Read each question carefully. Fill in the bubble next to your answer choice for each question.

1 If □ = 2, △ = 3, and ○ = 1, what is (□ × △) + ○ equal to?

○ A 7

○ B 6

○ C 5

○ D 4

2 What number does *x* stand for in the number sentence below?

$$20 \div x = 5$$

○ F 2

○ G 4

○ H 10

○ J 25

3 Dustin and Dena each counted how many baseball cards they have. They found that Dena has twice as many cards as Dustin plus 3 more. If *c* stands for the number of baseball cards that Dustin has, which of the following shows how many cards Dena has?

○ A $c \div 3 + 2$

○ B $3 \times c + 2$

○ C $2 \times c + 3$

○ D $2 \times c - 3$

4 What number does □ stand for?

□ × (6 − 3) = 6

○ F 9

○ G 7

○ H 3

○ J 2

5 Mary Beth likes to play softball even more than Bobbi Jo. Mary Beth has played in 3 times as many games as Bobbi Jo. If *G* represents the number of games Bobbi Jo has played, which of the following shows how many *more* games Mary Beth has played?

○ A $3 \times G$

○ B $3 \times G + G$

○ C $G - G + G$

○ D $3 \times G - G$

Don't let symbols and letters confuse you. When you see one in a math problem, remind yourself that the symbol or letter is really a number. If you solve the problem, you can turn the symbol back into the number it stands for.

MILE 44: VARIABLES AS WORDS

When you don't know the value of a number, you can use a *variable* to represent it. You can add, subtract, multiply, and divide the variable just as you can any number.

Examples:

x is a number for which the value you do not know.
$x + 5$ is "5 more than the number."

Directions: The phrases in the left column represent expressions. Match the phrase in the left column with the expression in the right column that contains the same information.

1. ______	five more than a number	A)	$2 \times q$
2. ______	three times a number	B)	$w - 7$
3. ______	six less than a number	C)	$3 \times a$
4. ______	a number divided by eight	D)	$2 \div y$
5. ______	seven times a number	E)	$5 + x$
6. ______	double a number	F)	$7 \times f$
7. ______	four less than a number	G)	$6 \times d$
8. ______	nine divided by a number	H)	$y - 4$
9. ______	one less than a number	I)	$9 \div p$
10. ______	four divided by a number	J)	$h + 1$
11. ______	four times a number	K)	$b \div 8$
12. ______	two divided by a number	L)	$4 \div m$
13. ______	eight more than a number	M)	$b + 8$
14. ______	a number divided by five	N)	$x \div 5$
15. ______	six times a number	O)	$z - 6$
16. ______	a number divided by two	P)	$x \times 9$
17. ______	one more than a number	Q)	$x - 1$
18. ______	two more than a number	R)	$b + 2$
19. ______	seven less than a number	S)	$4 \times k$
20. ______	nine times a number	T)	$s \div 2$

Directions: Read each question carefully. Fill in the bubble next to your answer choice for each question.

1 Which has the same meaning as $x + 4$, if x represents a number?

○ A Four more than a number

○ B Four less than a number

○ C Four times a number

○ D Four divided by a number

2 Which expression has the same meaning as "three times a number" when d represents the number?

○ F $d - 3$

○ G $d + 3$

○ H $d \div 3$

○ J $d \times 3$

3 Which has the same meaning as $y \times 7$, if y represents a number?

○ A Seven more than a number

○ B Seven less than a number

○ C Seven times a number

○ D Seven divided by a number

4 Which expression has the same meaning as "two less than a number" when w represents the number?

○ F $w + 2$

○ G $2 + w$

○ H $w - 2$

○ J $2 - w$

5 Which phrase has the same meaning as $8 \div a$, if a represents a number that is not 0?

○ A Eight more than a number

○ B Eight less than a number

○ C Eight times a number

○ D Eight divided by a number

Remember that when you add two numbers, the result is more than either of the two numbers. When you subtract numbers, the result is less than the first number in the subtraction number sentence. If you remember these two things, you should have no trouble translating variable expressions into words.

Mile 45: Open Sentences

Open sentences use variables, operations, and numbers to solve problems. The variable in an open sentence represents the value for which you are trying to solve. You can write an open sentence for any problem that has an unknown variable.

Example:

Arthur had x miniature automobiles. After his friend Laverne gave him 5 more miniature automobiles, Arthur had 20 miniature automobiles. How many miniature automobiles did Arthur have before he received Laverne's gift?

To solve this problem, write this open sentence and solve for x.

$$x + 5 = 20$$

Therefore, $x = 15$

Directions: Read each problem and then write an open sentence that could be used to solve it. You don't need to solve the problems!

1. Sharon sold W items at the annual Barnum Street Yard Sale. Her neighbor Bill sold 20 items, which is twice as many as Sharon sold. How many items did Sharon sell at the yard sale?

   ____

2. Vince can run a mile in exactly M minutes. His friend Barbara can run a mile in 1 minute less than Vince can. It takes Barbara 7 minutes to run a mile. How long does it take Vince to run a mile?

   ____

3. On the Fourth of July, Olson's Bakery handed out C cupcakes to 20 children who visited the bakery. Each of the children received 2 cupcakes. How many cupcakes did Olson's Bakery hand out on the Fourth of July?

   ____

4. Milo received a score of Y on his history test. His friend Joan received a score of 82, which was 5 points lower than Milo's score. What score did Milo receive on the history test?

   ____

5. Alan has a collection of Z baseball cards. His friend Louis has 270 baseball cards. When they combine their collections, they have 640 baseball cards all together. How many baseball cards are in Alan's collection?

   ____

Directions: Read each question carefully. Fill in the bubble next to your answer choice for each question.

1 $55 \div 5 = K$

Which problem can be solved using this open number sentence?

○ **A** A school club had 55 members. Then 5 new members joined. What is K, the number of club members after the new members joined?

○ **B** The school library bought 5 copies of 55 different books. What is K, the total number of books the library bought?

○ **C** Fifty-five students were supposed to go on a field trip. On the day of the trip, however, 5 students were absent from school. What is K, the number of students who went on the field trip?

○ **D** There is a total of 55 students in 5 classrooms. If there is an equal number of students in each classroom, what is K, the number of students in each classroom?

2 **Vanessa wrote a 5-page report. She then made 4 photocopies of the report. Which number sentence would help you find X, the number of photocopied pages Vanessa ended up with?**

○ **F** $5 \times 4 = X$

○ **G** $X + 4 = 5$

○ **H** $5 - 4 = X$

○ **J** $4 \div X = 5$

3 **Daryl grows tomato plants. On the first day of the month, one of Daryl's plants had 6 tomatoes growing on it. By the fifteenth day of the month, the number of tomatoes on the tomato plant had doubled. Which number sentence would help you find T, the number of tomatoes on the tomato plant on the fifteenth day of the month?**

○ **A** $6 + 2 = T$

○ **B** $6 \times 2 = T$

○ **C** $6 \div 2 = T$

○ **D** $6 \times T = 2$

You will be able to solve some open sentence questions easily. If you can solve the question, you can test the answer choices by replacing the variables with your solution. All of the incorrect answer choices will result in untrue number sentences. Only the answer choice that results in a true sentence can be the correct one.

PRACTICE TEST 1

Introduction to the Practice Tests

You've finished all of the miles in this book. That means you've practiced all of the important fifth-grade math skills. Way to go!

If you want to check your answers to questions in the miles, turn to page 141. All of the correct answers are on pages 143 to 163.

Now it's time to take the practice tests. The practice tests in this book are similar to the grade five Virginia SOL math test.

On the actual Virginia SOL math test, you will answer the questions on a separate answer sheet. You will have to fill in bubbles with a pencil to show your answers.

How to Take the Practice Tests

The answer sheet for Practice Test 1 is on the next page. The answer sheet for Practice Test 2 is on page 125. That's right before Practice Test 2 begins. Before you take each practice test, you should tear or cut out the answer sheet that goes with it.

Try to take each practice test as if it were the actual Virginia SOL test. That means you should not have any books open while taking these tests. You will not be allowed to use a calculator on section 1 of the actual test, but you can use one while completing section 2 of the test. You will be allowed to use scratch paper and a ruler that measures inches and centimeters during the test. You should definitely use them when taking these practice tests.

Take one whole practice test at a time. If you begin a practice test, don't stop until you are finished. Because the Virginia SOL math test is untimed, you can take as much time as you need to finish each practice test. Do not watch television, talk on the phone, or listen to music when you take these tests.

Remember to use the tips and skills that you have learned and practiced in this book. They will help you to do your best. After you have taken each test, have an adult go over it. The answers and explanations to the practice tests begin on page 165. Read the explanations of the correct answers for as many questions as you need. Pay special attention to the explanations of questions that you answered incorrectly or had difficulty answering.

Good luck!

Practice Test 1 Answer Sheet

Completely darken bubbles with a No. 2 pencil. If you make a mistake, be sure to erase mark completely. Erase all stray marks.

1. YOUR NAME: ____
(Print) Last First M.I.

SIGNATURE: ______________________________ **DATE:** ___ / ___ / ___

HOME ADDRESS: ____
(Print) Number

____
City State Zip Code

PHONE NO.: ____
(Print)

2. YOUR NAME

First 4 letters of last name				FIRST INIT	MID INIT
A	A	A	A	A	A
B	B	B	B	B	B
C	C	C	C	C	C
D	D	D	D	D	D
E	E	E	E	E	E
F	F	F	F	F	F
G	G	G	G	G	G
H	H	H	H	H	H
I	I	I	I	I	I
J	J	J	J	J	J
K	K	K	K	K	K
L	L	L	L	L	L
M	M	M	M	M	M
N	N	N	N	N	N
O	O	O	O	O	O
P	P	P	P	P	P
Q	Q	Q	Q	Q	Q
R	R	R	R	R	R
S	S	S	S	S	S
T	T	T	T	T	T
U	U	U	U	U	U
V	V	V	V	V	V
W	W	W	W	W	W
X	X	X	X	X	X
Y	Y	Y	Y	Y	Y
Z	Z	Z	Z	Z	Z

3. DATE OF BIRTH

Month	Day		Year			
JAN						
FEB						
MAR	0	0	0	0	0	0
APR	1	1	1	1	1	1
MAY	2	2	2	2	2	2
JUN	3	3	3	3	3	3
JUL		4	4	4	4	4
AUG		5	5	5	5	5
SEP		6	6	6	6	6
OCT		7	7	7	7	7
NOV		8	8	8	8	8
DEC		9	9	9	9	9

The Princeton Review

4. SEX

- MALE
- FEMALE

Practice Test 1 — Calculator Inactive

1. A B C D
2. F G H J
3. A B C D
4. F G H J
5. A B C D
6. F G H J
7. A B C D
8. F G H J
9. A B C D
10. F G H J
11. A B C D
12. F G H J
13. A B C D
14. F G H J

Practice Test 1 — Calculator Active

15. A B C D
16. F G H J
17. A B C D
18. F G H J
19. A B C D
20. F G H J
21. A B C D
22. F G H J
23. A B C D
24. F G H J
25. A B C D
26. F G H J
27. A B C D
28. F G H J
29. A B C D
30. F G H J
31. A B C D
32. F G H J
33. A B C D
34. F G H J
35. A B C D
36. F G H J
37. A B C D
38. F G H J
39. A B C D
40. F G H J
41. A B C D
42. F G H J
43. A B C D
44. F G H J
45. A B C D
46. F G H J
47. A B C D
48. F G H J
49. A B C D
50. F G H J
51. A B C D
52. F G H J
53. A B C D
54. F G H J
55. A B C D
56. F G H J
57. A B C D
58. F G H J
59. A B C D
60. F G H J

SECTION 1

Note: Calculator usage is not allowed for this section.

1 **A group of thirty-six local businesspeople donated a total of $6,372 to help pay for a new park. If each businessperson donated the same amount of money, how much did each one donate?**

A $6,336.00

B $1,296.00

C $177.00

D $17.77

2 **$0.4 \times 8.3 =$**

F 0.332

G 3.32

H 3.78

J 3.94

3 **Which answer is closest to 13,321 + 6,658?**

A 25,000

B 20,000

C 18,000

D 16,000

4 **$\frac{1}{8} + \frac{5}{8} =$**

F $\frac{1}{4}$

G $\frac{5}{16}$

H $\frac{6}{16}$

J $\frac{3}{4}$

5

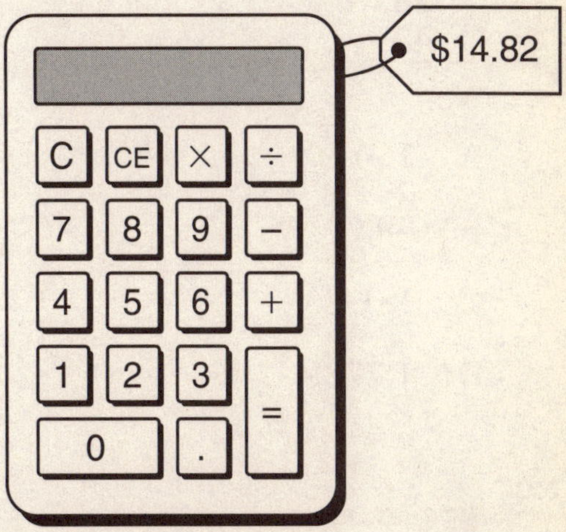

Andrea purchased this calculator with a $20 bill. How much change should the sales clerk have returned to her?

A $6.18

B $5.18

C $4.82

D $4.28

Go to next page

6 $8\frac{7}{8} - 2\frac{3}{8} =$

F $\frac{1}{2}$

G $4\frac{2}{3}$

H $6\frac{3}{4}$

J $6\frac{1}{2}$

7 $\begin{array}{r} 26 \\ \times\ 42 \\ \hline \end{array}$

A 156

B 892

C 1,092

D 1,772

8

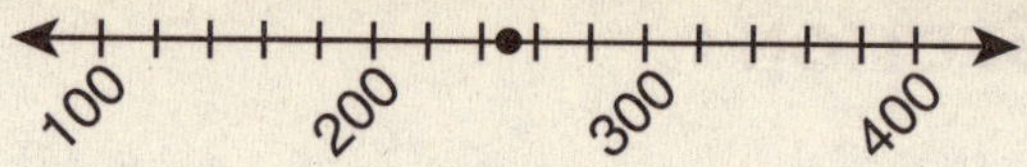

Which answer choice is closest to the value shown by the point on the number line?

F 504 ÷ 2

G 70 × 12

H 218 + 107

J 413 – 127

9 **3.6 × 7.2 =**

A 25.34

B 25.52

C 25.92

D 32.22

Go to next page

10

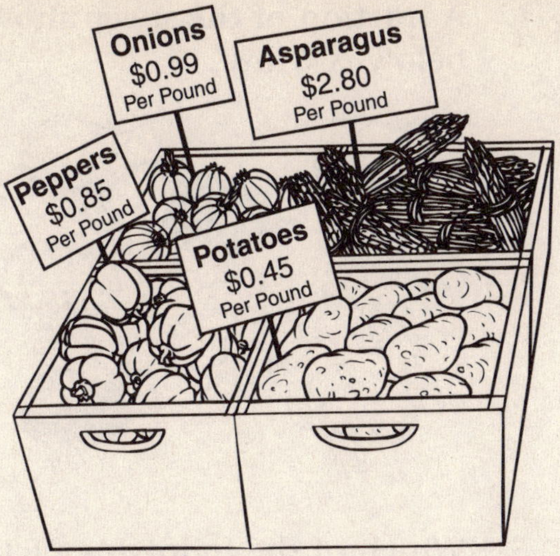

Milo takes $5 to the grocery store. If he buys a pound of asparagus, what else can he buy?

F 3 pounds of onions

G 4 pounds of peppers

H 1 pound of potatoes, 1 pound of onions, and 1 pound of peppers

J 3 pounds of potatoes and 1 pound of peppers

11 **2,940 ÷ 12 =**

A 255

B 245

C 240 R6

D 211 R8

12 $$\begin{array}{r} \frac{5}{6} \\ +\ \frac{1}{3} \\ \hline \end{array}$$

F $\frac{6}{9}$

G 1

H $1\frac{1}{6}$

J $1\frac{1}{3}$

13 $4\overline{)0.952}$

A 0.00238

B 0.0238

C 0.238

D 2.38

14 **A crate holds 24 jars of homemade jam. Phil has 192 jars of homemade jam. How many crates will he need to store his jam?**

F 4,608

G 216

H 8

J $\frac{1}{8}$

Go to next page

Section 2

Note: Calculator usage is allowed for this section.

15 Which statement is correct?

A 0.45 < 0.4

B 0.681 < 0.6394

C 0.5187 < 0.53

D 0.9172 < 0.9052

16 This bag of marbles contains black, white, and gray marbles. The drawing shows how many of each type of marble is in the bag.

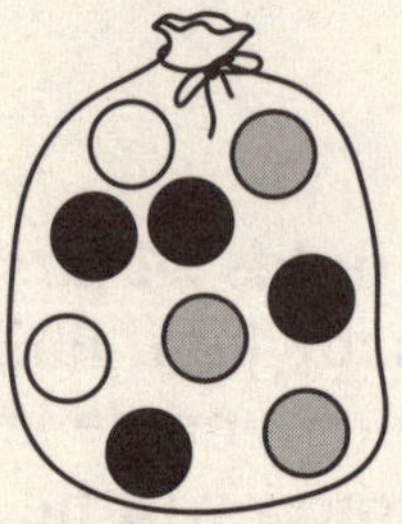

Without looking, Raya reaches into the bag and selects one marble. What is the probability that the marble she selects will be white?

F $\frac{2}{9}$

G $\frac{1}{4}$

H $\frac{2}{7}$

J $\frac{2}{3}$

17 A fraction of the sheep shown below is white.

Which of the following pictures shows an equivalent fraction of white sheep?

A 

B 

C 

D 

Go to next page

18 A highway patrol officer measured the speed, in miles per hour (mph), of six cars traveling on a highway. The speeds of the cars are listed below.

56 mph	58 mph	66 mph
64 mph	66 mph	56 mph

What was the mean (average) speed of the six cars?

F 65 mph

G 64 mph

H 62 mph

J 61 mph

19 Vernon uses dot patterns to create these triangles.

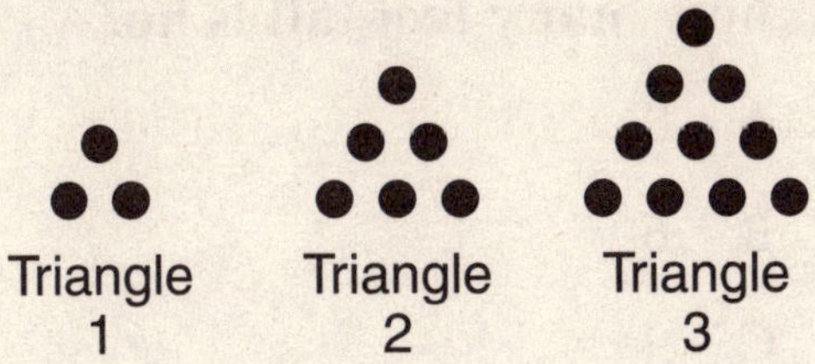

If the pattern continues, how many dots will Vernon use to create Triangle 4?

A 11

B 13

C 15

D 16

20 The shaded part of this model represents a decimal value. What value does it represent?

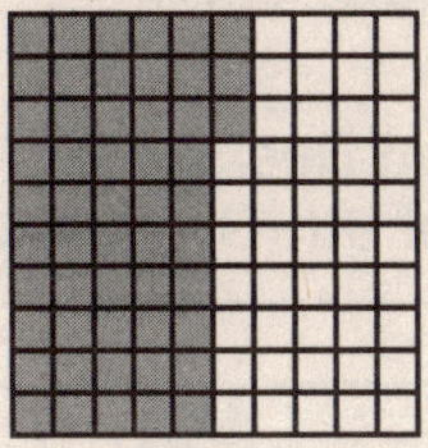

F 53.3

G 5.3

H 5.03

J 0.53

21 The length of each side of a square is 6 feet. What is the area of the square?

A 12 $feet^2$

B 18 $feet^2$

C 24 $feet^2$

D 36 $feet^2$

Go to next page

22 This graph shows the number of students who voted for each of the four candidates in the election for president of a fifth-grade class.

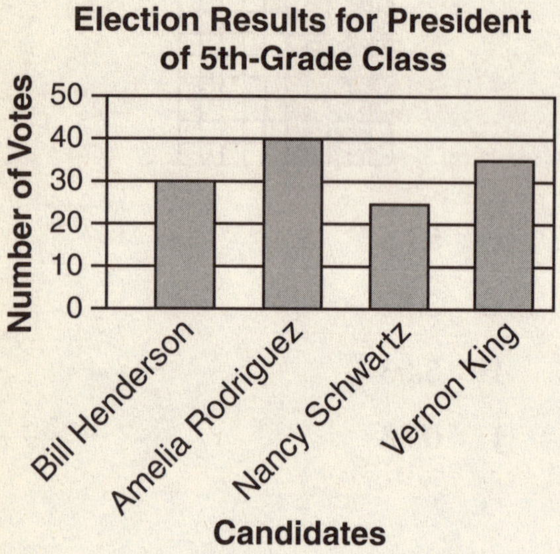

Which candidate received twenty-five votes?

F Bill Henderson

G Amelia Rodriguez

H Nancy Schwartz

J Vernon King

23 "Seven and one hundred fifty-three ten-thousandths" is the same as —

A 7.000153

B 7.0153

C 7.153

D 7,153.00

24 This table shows the height of different stairways.

Number of Steps	Height in Feet
5	3.75
6	4.5
7	5.25
8	6

If the pattern shown in the table continues, what would be the height of a stairway with ten steps?

F 7.5 feet

G 7 feet

H 6.75 feet

J 6.25 feet

25 Charles is 2 meters tall. About how many feet tall is he?

A 3

B 6

C 9

D 12

26 The fraction $\frac{1}{2}$ is greater than which fraction?

F $\frac{3}{5}$

G $\frac{4}{10}$

H $\frac{5}{6}$

J $\frac{5}{8}$

Go to next page

27

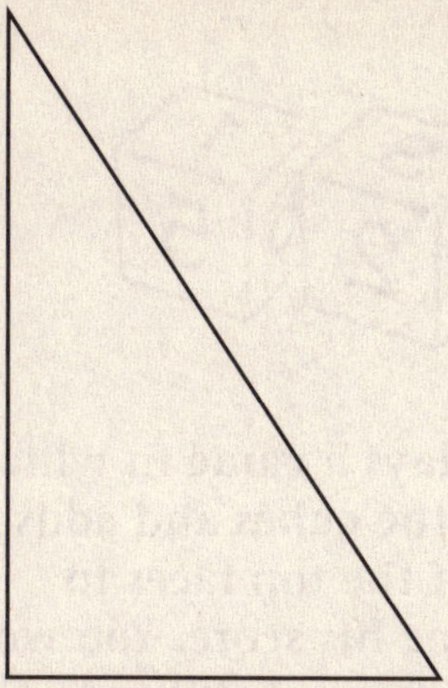

You will need to use your centimeter ruler to answer this question. The perimeter of this triangle is most nearly —

A 17 centimeters

B 15 centimeters

C 12 inches

D 7 inches

28 **In which situation would you need to know the area of something?**

F You want to know how much water it takes to fill a swimming pool.

G You want to buy enough carpet to cover a floor.

H You want to build a fence around your backyard.

J You want to buy enough ribbon to wrap a gift package.

29 **These shapes create a pattern.**

If the pattern continues, what will the 7th shape in the pattern look like?

A 

B 

C 

D 

Go to next page

30 Tamara lives 7.18 miles from her friend Linda. What is this distance rounded to the nearest tenth?

F 7.2 miles

G 7.1 miles

H 7.08 miles

J 7.01 miles

31

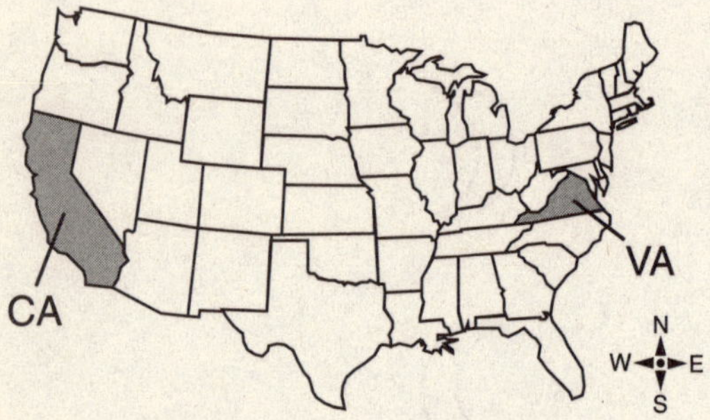

The distance from California to Virginia would best be measured in —

A feet

B inches

C gallons

D miles

32 David has two number cubes.

David plays a game in which he rolls the cubes and adds the values of the top faces to determine his score. You would need to use probability to find the answer to which question?

F What is the likelihood that David will score a 7 on one roll?

G What is the highest possible score David could receive on one roll?

H How many faces have even numbers on them?

J How many faces does each number cube have?

33 A school assembly began at 11:15 A.M. and ended at 12:40 P.M. How long did the assembly last?

A 1 hour, 25 minutes

B 1 hour, 35 minutes

C 2 hours, 25 minutes

D 23 hours, 55 minutes

Go to next page

34 **Which line segment shows the radius of the circle with its center at point *X*?**

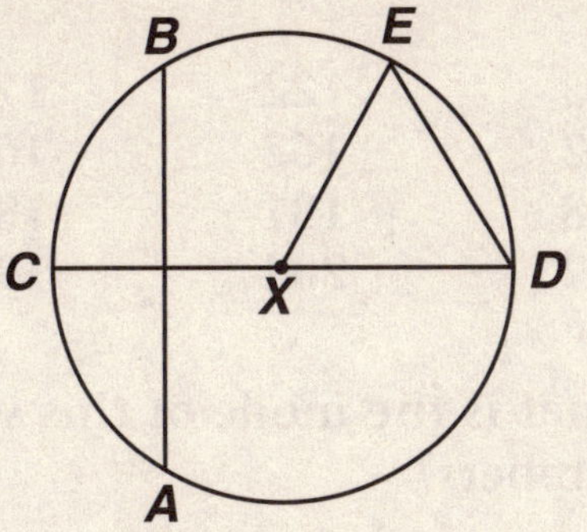

F Line segment *AB*

G Line segment *CD*

H Line segment *DE*

J Line segment *XE*

35 **Which statement is correct?**

A 539,580 > 546,210

B 568,418 > 570,198

C 564,535 > 546,107

D 583,524 > 596,213

36 **Choose the answer that makes this statement true.**

All right triangles have —

F two equal sides

G three equal sides

H one angle that equals 90°

J two angles that equal 90° each

37 **There are 182 boys and girls who signed up to play in a baseball league. The league plans to create fourteen teams. Each team is to have the same number of players. Which number sentence should the league officials use to figure out how many players should be on each team?**

A $182 \div 14 = 13$

B $182 \times 14 = 2{,}548$

C $182 + 14 = 196$

D $182 - 14 = 168$

Go to next page

38 **Chet has a coin with one side that shows "heads" and another side that shows "tails." He tosses the coin twice. Which diagram shows all the possible results of the two tosses of the coin?**

F 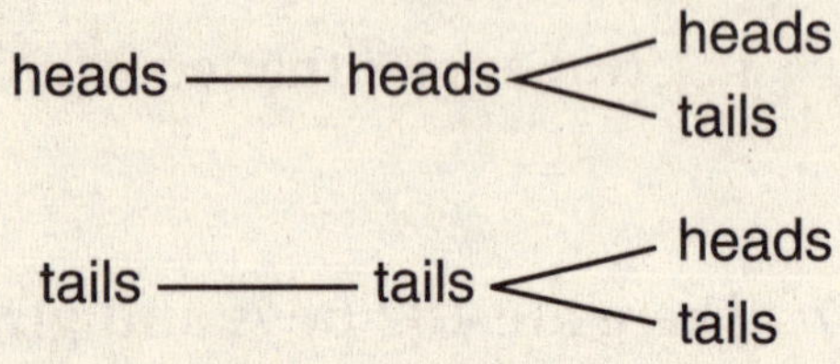

G 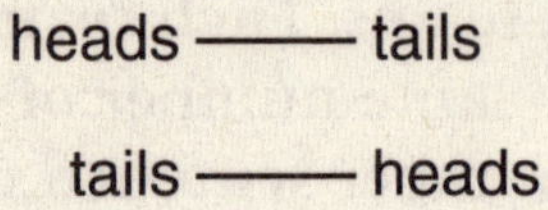

H 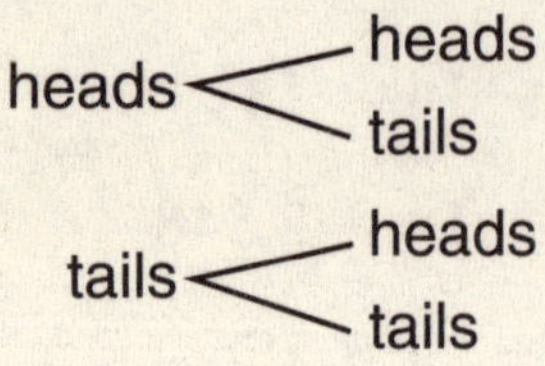

J 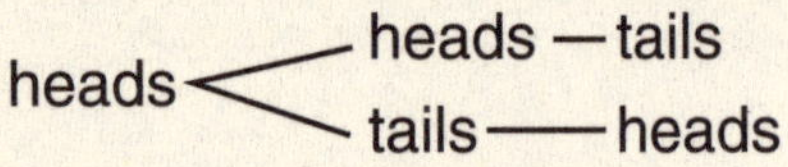

39 **Mollie went bowling four days in a row. Each day she bowled three games. This list shows her scores for the twelve games she bowled.**

145	122	177
162	162	162
138	181	181
202	204	199

What is the mode of this set of numbers?

A 204

B 177

C 165.35

D 162

40 **Which answer choice shows the number "twelve and five one-hundredths"?**

F 12.05

G 12.5

H 120.5

J 1,205

Go to next page

41 This line graph shows the population of the state of Virginia between the years 1990 and 1998.

Population of the State of Virginia 1990–1998

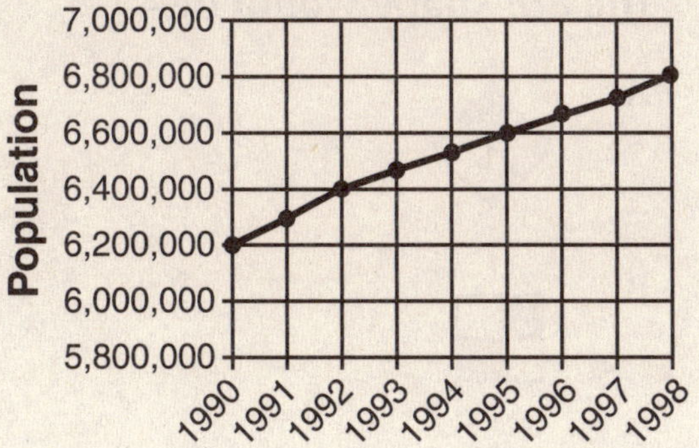

The population of the state of Virginia in 1991 was approximately —

A 6,500,000

B 6,400,000

C 6,300,000

D 6,200,000

42

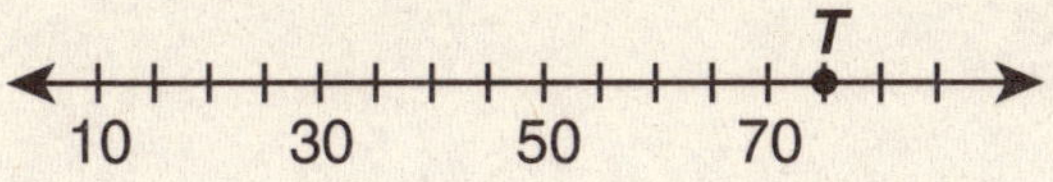

What is the value of point *T* on this number line?

F 71

G 73

H 75

J 85

43 Which number sentence is true when $X = 8$?

A $7 \times X = 15$

B $40 \div X = 5$

C $24 - X = 4$

D $X + 5 = 3$

44 A fraction of this square is black.

Which figure has the same fractional part shaded?

F 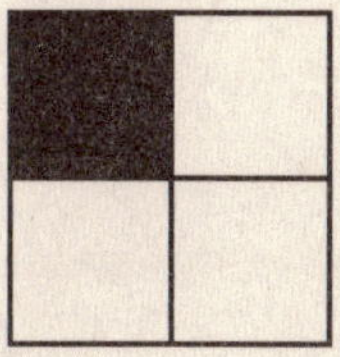

G 

H 

J 

Go to next page

45 This stem-and-leaf plot shows the high temperatures for ten consecutive days in June.

High Temperatures

Stem	Leaf
7	1, 1, 4, 8
8	3, 5, 5, 8, 9
9	2

Which list shows the same data as the stem-and-leaf plot?

A 74, 78, 83, 85, 88, 89, 92

B 78, 79, 87, 89, 97, 98

C 71, 74, 78, 83, 85, 87, 88, 89, 92, 98

D 71, 71, 74, 78, 83, 85, 85, 88, 89, 92

46

You will need to use your centimeter ruler to answer this question. What is the sum of the lengths of all four lines used to draw the letter W?

F $6\frac{1}{2}$ centimeters

G 7 centimeters

H 8 centimeters

J $9\frac{1}{2}$ centimeters

47 These shapes create a pattern.

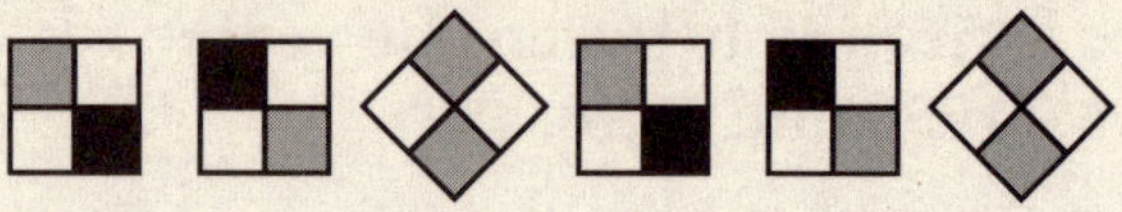

If the pattern were to continue, the *8th* shape would be —

A

B

C

D

Go to next page

48

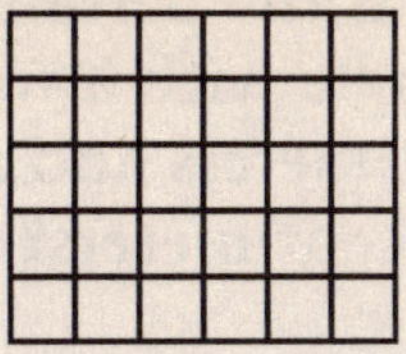

Which of the following statements is true about this figure?

F Its area is 11 and its perimeter is 22.

G Its area is 30 and its perimeter is 9.

H Its area is 25 and its perimeter is 18.

J Its area is 30 and its perimeter is 22.

49 Andrea runs fifteen laps around the school track every day for seven days in a row. To figure out the value of *L*, the number of laps Andrea ran during the entire seven-day period, you should use the number sentence —

A $15 + 7 = L$

B $15 \times 7 = L$

C $15 - 7 = L$

D $7 \times L = 15$

50 Which shows an acute angle?

F

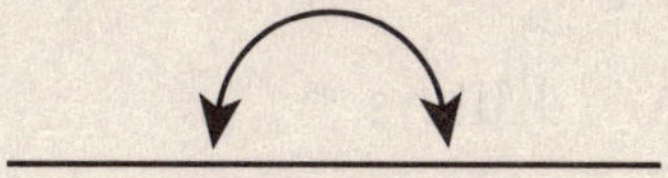

G

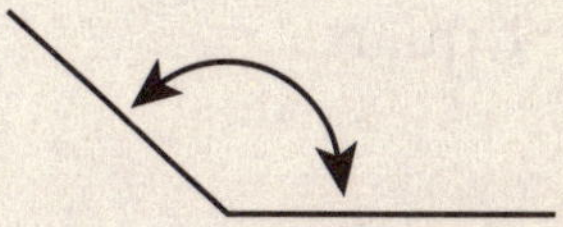

H

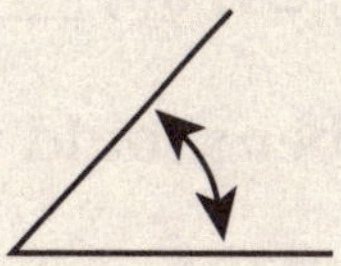

J

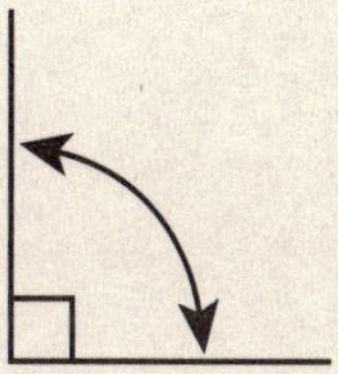

Go to next page

51 Ms. Hernandez filled her lawn mower with 1 gallon of gasoline. Which measure is closest to the amount of gasoline she used?

A 4 liters

B 4 pints

C 4 cups

D 1 quart

52 These numbers form a pattern.

6, 9, 12, 18, 24, 36, ___

What number should fill the blank?

F 48

G 54

H 60

J 78

53 Which expression has the same meaning as "eight less than a number" when y represents the number?

A $y \times 8$

B $y \div 8$

C $y + 8$

D $y - 8$

54 What is the perimeter of a rectangle with a width of 7 centimeters and a length of 12 centimeters?

F 19 cm

G 38 cm

H 42 cm

J 84 cm

55 This spinner is divided into equal parts. Each part is white, black, or gray.

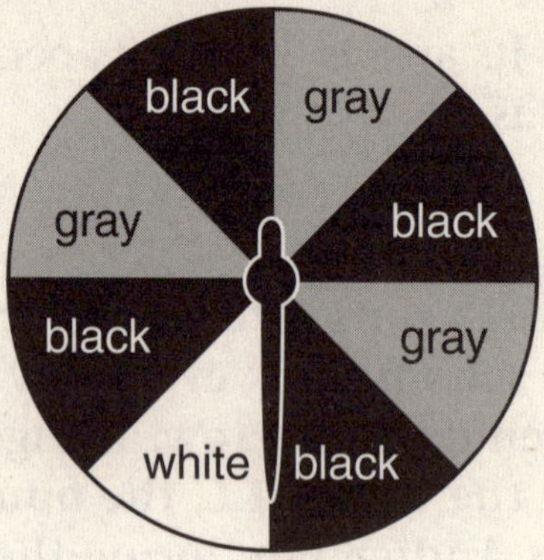

What is the probability that the spinner will land on a black space?

A $\frac{3}{4}$

B $\frac{2}{3}$

C $\frac{1}{2}$

D $\frac{1}{3}$

Go to next page

56 $X \times 2 = ?$

Which problem can be solved using this open number sentence?

F There are two more cats on a couch than there are on an armchair. If X is the number of cats on the couch, how many cats are on the armchair?

G A farmer sold half the cows on his farm. If X is the number of cows he had before the sale, how many cows did the farmer have after the sale?

H Two fish tanks contain the same number of fish. If X is the number of fish in one fish tank, how many fish are in both fish tanks?

J Steven has two fewer rabbits than Vincent has. If X is the number of rabbits Vincent has, how many rabbits does Steven have?

57 **There are four boys and three girls in this study group.**

How can you express the number of boys in this group as a fraction?

A $\frac{3}{7}$

B $\frac{4}{7}$

C $\frac{2}{4}$

D $\frac{4}{3}$

58 **Every year on his birthday, Donovan records his weight. The table below shows how much Donovan weighed on his 8th, 9th, 10th, and 11th birthdays.**

Birthday	Weight
8	55 pounds
9	63 pounds
10	74 pounds
11	87 pounds

Which line graph shows the same data as this table?

F

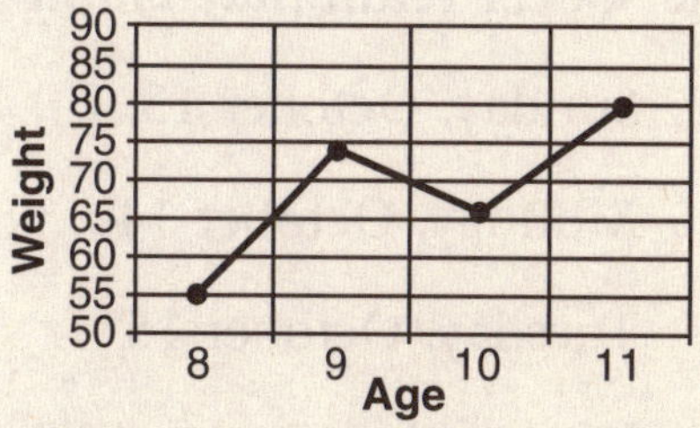

G

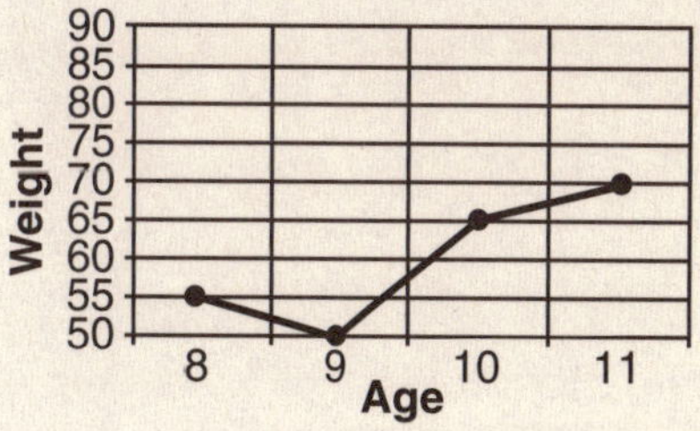

H

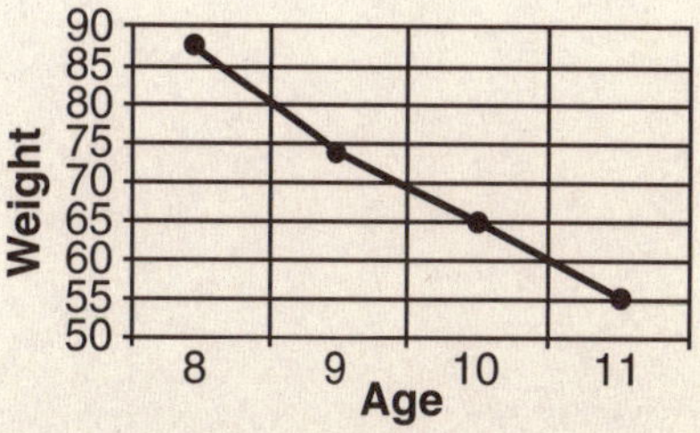

J

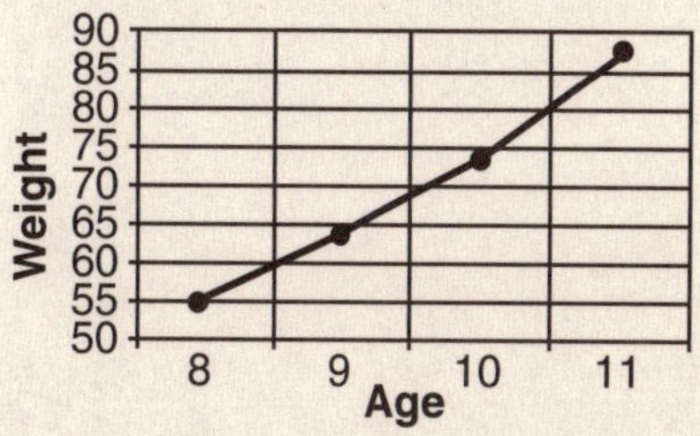

Go to next page

59 **This calendar shows part of a schedule for a soccer team.**

OCTOBER						
SUN	MON	TUE	WED	THU	FRI	SAT
		1 Game #1	2 No Game	3 No Game	4 Game #2	5 No Game
6 No Game	7 Game #3	8 No Game	9 No Game	10 Game #4	11 No Game	12 No Game
13	14	15	16	17	18	19

If the pattern shown on the schedule continues, when will the soccer team play Game #6?

A Sunday, October 13

B Monday, October 14

C Tuesday, October 15

D Wednesday, October 16

60 **The distance around a circle is called its —**

F circumference

G radius

H diameter

J area

STOP

Practice Test 2

PRACTICE TEST 2 ANSWER SHEET

Completely darken bubbles with a No. 2 pencil. If you make a mistake, be sure to erase mark completely. Erase all stray marks.

1. YOUR NAME: ______________________________
(Print) Last First M.I.

SIGNATURE: ______________________ **DATE:** ___/___/___

HOME ADDRESS: ______________________________
(Print) Number

____
City State Zip Code

PHONE NO.: ______________________________
(Print)

2. YOUR NAME

First 4 letters of last name				FIRST INIT	MID INIT
A	A	A	A	A	A
B	B	B	B	B	B
C	C	C	C	C	C
D	D	D	D	D	D
E	E	E	E	E	E
F	F	F	F	F	F
G	G	G	G	G	G
H	H	H	H	H	H
I	I	I	I	I	I
J	J	J	J	J	J
K	K	K	K	K	K
L	L	L	L	L	L
M	M	M	M	M	M
N	N	N	N	N	N
O	O	O	O	O	O
P	P	P	P	P	P
Q	Q	Q	Q	Q	Q
R	R	R	R	R	R
S	S	S	S	S	S
T	T	T	T	T	T
U	U	U	U	U	U
V	V	V	V	V	V
W	W	W	W	W	W
X	X	X	X	X	X
Y	Y	Y	Y	Y	Y
Z	Z	Z	Z	Z	Z

3. DATE OF BIRTH

Month	Day		Year			
JAN						
FEB						
MAR	0	0	0	0	0	0
APR	1	1	1	1	1	1
MAY	2	2	2	2	2	2
JUN	3	3	3	3	3	3
JUL		4	4	4	4	4
AUG		5	5	5	5	5
SEP		6	6	6	6	6
OCT		7	7	7	7	7
NOV		8	8	8	8	8
DEC		9	9	9	9	9

The Princeton Review

4. SEX

MALE
FEMALE

Practice Test 2 Calculator Inactive

1. A B C D	4. F G H J	7. A B C D	10. F G H J	13. A B C D
2. F G H J	5. A B C D	8. F G H J	11. A B C D	14. F G H J
3. A B C D	6. F G H J	9. A B C D	12. F G H J	

Practice Test 2 Calculator Active

15. A B C D	24. F G H J	33. A B C D	42. F G H J	51. A B C D
16. F G H J	25. A B C D	34. F G H J	43. A B C D	52. F G H J
17. A B C D	26. F G H J	35. A B C D	44. F G H J	53. A B C D
18. F G H J	27. A B C D	36. F G H J	45. A B C D	54. F G H J
19. A B C D	28. F G H J	37. A B C D	46. F G H J	55. A B C D
20. F G H J	29. A B C D	38. F G H J	47. A B C D	56. F G H J
21. A B C D	30. F G H J	39. A B C D	48. F G H J	57. A B C D
22. F G H J	31. A B C D	40. F G H J	49. A B C D	58. F G H J
23. A B C D	32. F G H J	41. A B C D	50. F G H J	59. A B C D
				60. F G H J

SECTION 1

Note: Calculator usage is not allowed for this section.

1 **Which is the best estimate of 49,036 – 8,975?**

A Slightly more than 35,000

B Slightly more than 40,000

C Slightly more than 45,000

D Slightly more than 50,000

2 $25\overline{)6{,}850}$

F 222

G 234

H 274

J 275 R10

3 $\begin{array}{r} 7.1 \\ \times\ 1.9 \\ \hline \end{array}$

A 1.349

B 13.29

C 13.44

D 13.49

4 $\frac{3}{5} + \frac{7}{10}$

F $4\frac{3}{10}$

G $\frac{2}{3}$

H $1\frac{3}{10}$

J 2

5

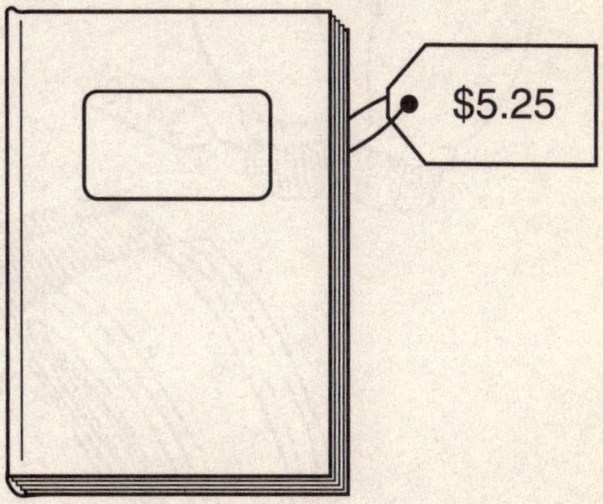

David has $20. What is the greatest number of copies of this book he can buy?

A 1

B 2

C 3

D 4

Go to next page

6 4,787 + 2,432 =

F 8,115

G 7,219

H 7,119

J 6,155

7

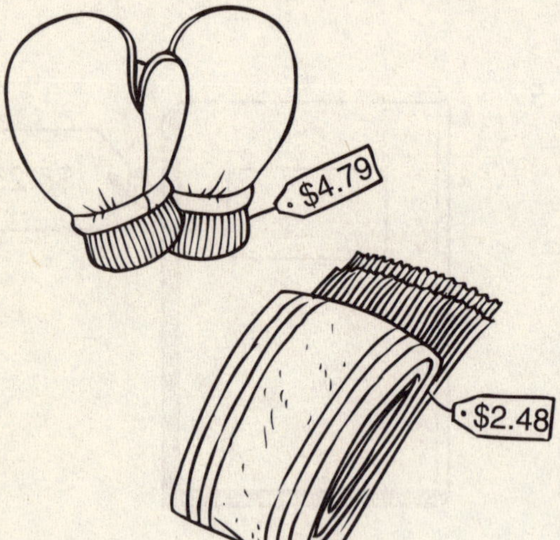

Melanie purchased a pair of mittens and a scarf. If she had $10.00 to pay for the items, how much change should have been returned to her?

A $3.83

B $3.73

C $2.83

D $2.73

8 Arthur and Audrey have 364 wooden boards. They plan to stack the boards in twenty-eight piles with an equal number of boards in each pile. How many boards will be in each pile?

F $1\frac{1}{3}$

G 13

H 392

J 10,192

9 $\frac{4}{12} + \frac{5}{12} =$

A $\frac{3}{4}$

B $\frac{3}{12}$

C $\frac{4}{12}$

C $\frac{20}{24}$

Go to next page

10 $0.516 \div 3 =$

F 0.0172

G 0.172

H 1.272

J 2.72

11

A portion of the number line above is shaded. Which result would fall within the shaded portion of the number line?

A $500 \div 4$

B $500 \div 100$

C 500×4

D 500×100

12 $\begin{array}{r} 24 \\ \times\ 58 \\ \hline \end{array}$

F 312

G 1,192

H 1,392

J 2,008

13 $5\frac{7}{9} - 4\frac{4}{9} =$

A $\frac{1}{9}$

B $\frac{2}{3}$

C $1\frac{1}{3}$

D $1\frac{1}{9}$

14 $0.5 + 2.2 + 29 =$

F 3.17

G 5.6

H 31.7

J 56.0

Go to next page

SECTION 2

Note: Calculator usage is allowed for this section.

15 Which statement is correct?

A $3.574 < 3.0574$

B $3.84 < 3.269$

C $3.7254 < 3.802$

D $3.241 < 3.240$

16 There are four boys and three girls in the French club.

One student is to be chosen at random to represent the club at a school meeting. What is the probability that the student will be a girl?

F $\frac{1}{4}$

G $\frac{3}{4}$

H $\frac{1}{7}$

J $\frac{3}{7}$

17 An obtuse angle is one that measures —

A exactly 90°

B less than 90°

C more than 90°

D less than 45°

18 These shapes form a pattern.

What will the *9th* circle look like if the pattern continues?

F 

G 

H 

J 

Go to next page

19 **Reese grew eight tomato plants. This table shows the number of tomatoes he harvested from each plant.**

Number of Tomatoes Harvested

Plant #1	8
Plant #2	10
Plant #3	13
Plant #4	9
Plant #5	5
Plant #6	13
Plant #7	7
Plant #8	11

The mode for the set of data shown above is —

A 9

B 9.5

C 10

D 13

20 **Brett walks 2 miles from home to school. About how many kilometers does he walk?**

F 0.5 kilometer

G 3 kilometers

H 12 kilometers

J 2,000 kilometers

21 **A rectangle has an area of 24 cm^2. Which of these could be the dimensions of the rectangle?**

A 4 cm by 3 cm

B 6 cm by 5 cm

C 8 cm by 2 cm

D 8 cm by 3 cm

22 **Which pair of circles has the same fractional part shaded?**

F 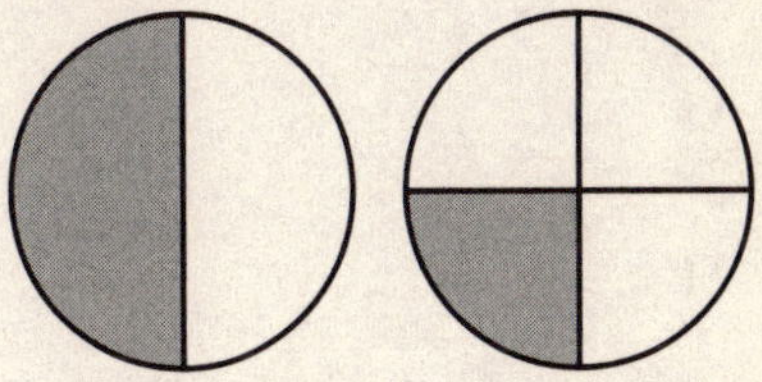

G 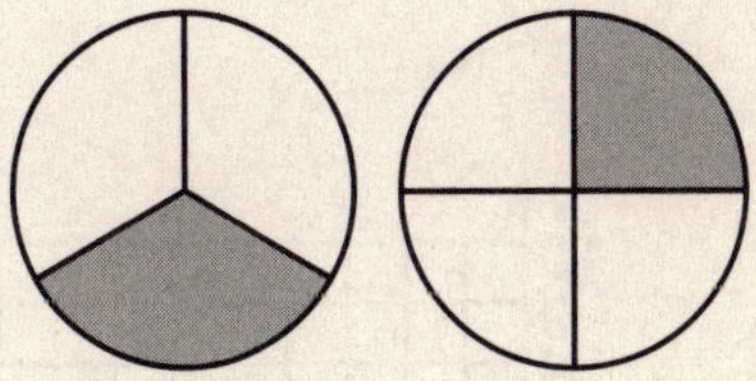

H 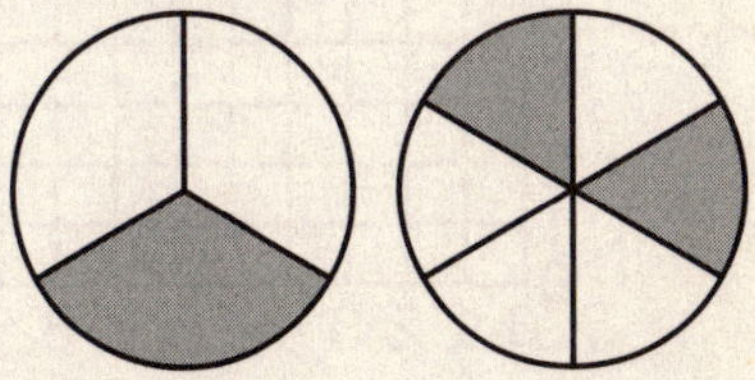

J 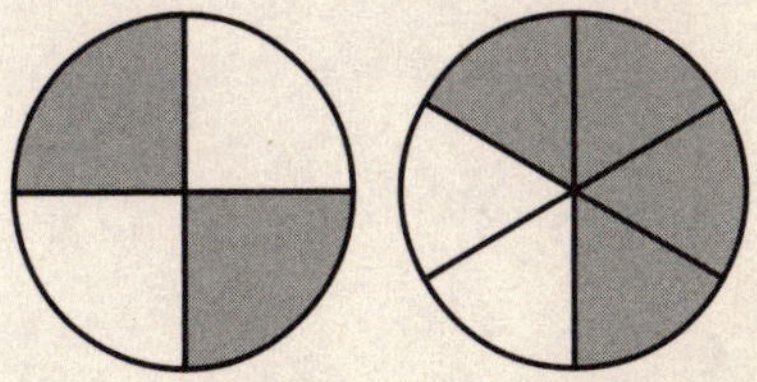

Go to next page

23 If 5 × *X* = 30, then what is the value of *X*?

A 5

B 6

C 10

D 15

24 Which fraction has the greatest value?

F $\frac{1}{3}$

G $\frac{1}{2}$

H $\frac{1}{6}$

J $\frac{1}{10}$

25

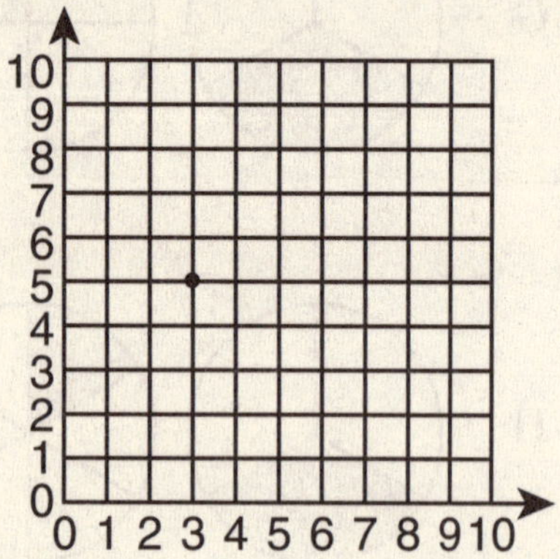

What are the coordinates of the point shown above?

A (3, 5)

B (5, 3)

C (3, 3)

D (0, 5)

26 This is a list of the weights, in pounds, of all the students in Ms. Dubrowski's class.

57	73	67	79	50	68
53	78	67	78	56	73
68	59	62	84	63	77

Which stem-and-leaf plot represents the same data?

F

Stem	Leaf
5	0, 3, 6, 7, 9
6	2, 3, 7, 8
7	3, 7, 8, 9
8	4

G

Stem	Leaf
5	3, 6, 7, 9
6	2, 3, 7, 7, 8
7	3, 3, 7, 8, 9
8	4

H

Stem	Leaf
5	0, 3, 6, 7, 9
6	0, 2, 3, 7, 7, 8
7	0, 3, 3, 7, 8, 9
8	0, 4

J

Stem	Leaf
5	0, 3, 6, 7, 9
6	2, 3, 7, 7, 8, 8
7	3, 3, 7, 8, 8, 9
8	4

Go to next page

27 **These numbers form a pattern.**

36, 45, 54, 63, ____, ____

Which numbers are missing from the pattern?

A 72, 81

B 71, 79

C 73, 84

D 73, 83

28 **The phrase "seven and one hundred-six ten-thousandths" is the same as which number?**

F 7.016

G 7.0106

H 7.16

J 7,106.00

29

Which unit would be best for measuring the weight of a cruise ship?

A Miles

B Pounds

C Tons

D Kilograms

30 **Janet began a nature hike at 10:45 A.M. Her hike ended at 1:16 P.M. How long was Janet's hike?**

F 3 hours and 45 minutes

G 3 hours and 1 minute

H 2 hours and 31 minutes

J 1 hour and 31 minutes

31 **Which of the following fractions is less than $\frac{2}{7}$?**

A $\frac{3}{12}$

B $\frac{1}{3}$

C $\frac{2}{5}$

D $\frac{4}{5}$

32 **This list shows the number of cakes sold at the Smiling Glutton Bakery on four consecutive days.**

35
42
29
46

What is the mean (average) number of cakes sold per day for those four days?

F 35

G 36

H 38

J 42

Go to next page

33 Alison teaches four swimming classes. Each class has eight students. Which expression could you use to determine *S*, the total number of students that Alison teaches?

A $8 + 4 = S$

B $S \times 8 = 4$

C $8 \times 4 = S$

D $8 \div 4 = S$

34 The table shows the prices of four popular computer games.

GAME	PRICE
Castle Climber	$28
Battle on Saturn	$34
Get Those Ducks!	$30
Extreme Football	$32

The mean (average) price of the four games is —

F $28

G $30

H $31

J $33

35 Look closely at this number pattern.

20, 26, 18, 24, 16, 22, 14, ____

If the pattern continues, what number will come next?

A 16

B 20

C 28

D 36

36 You will need a ruler to answer this question.

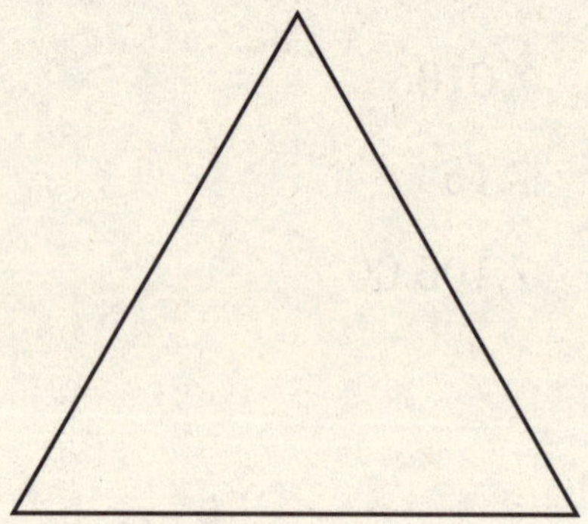

What is the perimeter of this triangle?

F 2 inches

G 3 inches

H 4 inches

J 6 inches

Go to next page

37 **A fractional part of this diamond is shaded gray.**

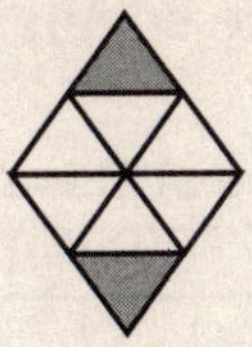

Which triangle has an equal fractional part shaded gray?

A 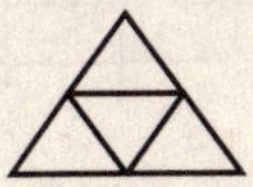

B 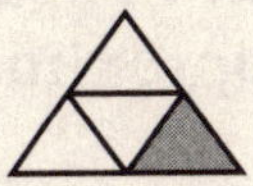

C 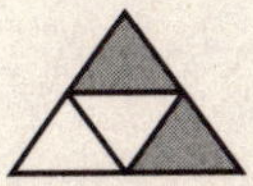

D 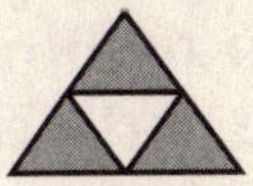

38 **Which decimal value has a 7 in the hundredths place?**

F 761.035

G 947.529

H 255.704

J 428.573

39 **Look at this open sentence.**

$$200 \times Y = 600$$

Which question can you answer using this open sentence?

A A business ran two hundred advertisements on each of six hundred radio stations. What is *Y*, the total number of advertisements the company ran on all six hundred radio stations?

B On Friday two hundred people attended a play. On Saturday, *Y* people attended the play. If six hundred people attended the play on Friday and Saturday combined, how many people attended the play on Saturday?

C A rancher divided two hundred buffalo into smaller herds. If there were *Y* buffalo in each new herd, into how many herds were the buffalo divided?

D Last year two hundred students donated money to a local charity. If each student gave *Y* dollars and the charity collected a total of $600 from the students, how much did each student donate?

Go to next page

40 This table shows the number of goals five field hockey players scored in a season.

Player	Goals
Brenda	12
Charlene	6
Deborah	10
Elizabeth	18
Fatima	10

Which bar graph shows the same information?

F 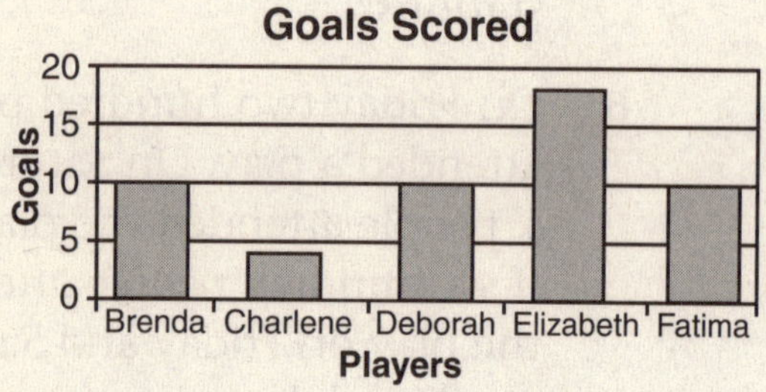

G 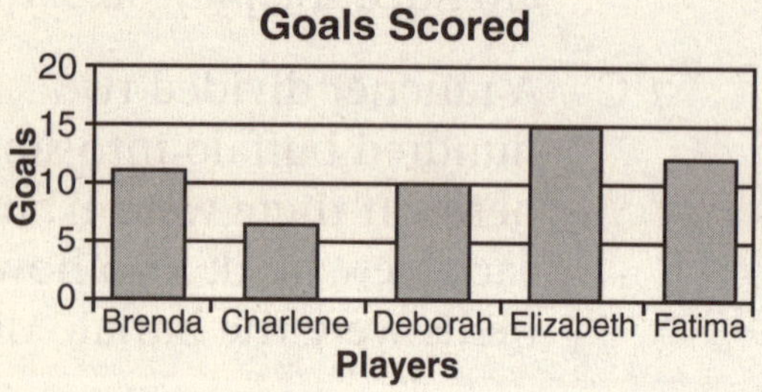

H 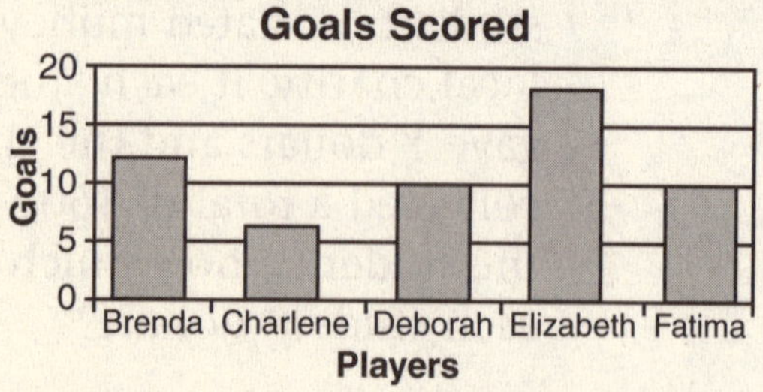

J 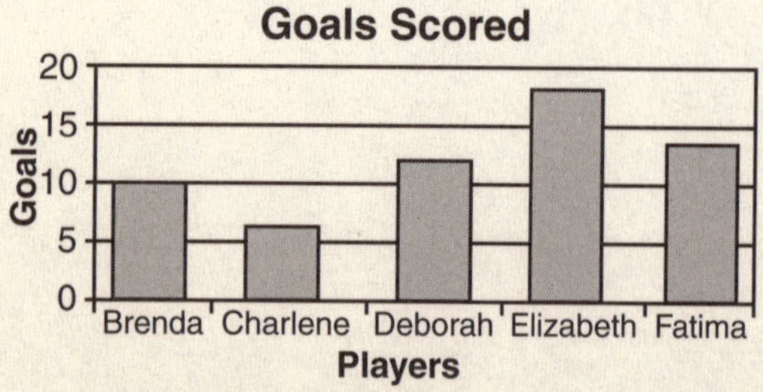

41 A baseball team played games on seven consecutive days. This graph shows the attendance at each of the seven games.

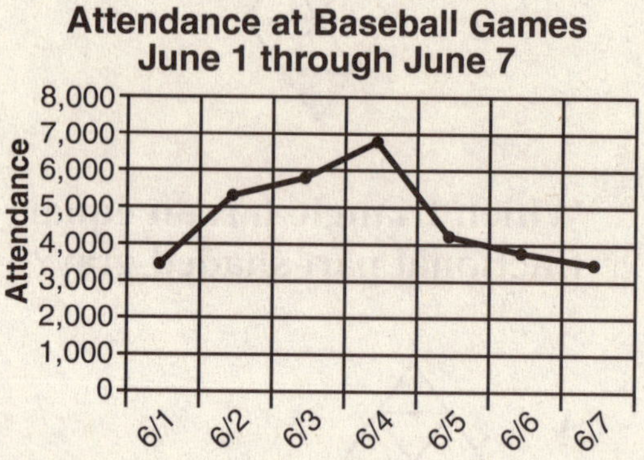

The attendance at the game played on June 2 was approximately —

A 3,700

B 4,100

C 5,200

D 6,800

42 Which question requires you to calculate the perimeter of an object?

F How much paint does Doris need to paint one wall of her bedroom?

G How much fencing does Billy need to completely surround his garden?

H How long does it take Andrea to ride her bicycle from her home to the library?

J How much milk does Henry's bucket hold?

Go to next page

43 **Which of the following is an obtuse triangle?**

A 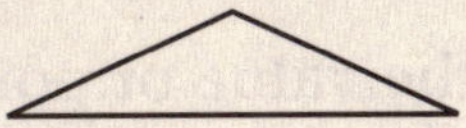

B 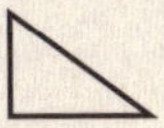

C 

D 

44 **Harlan is 1.476 meters tall. What is Harlan's height, rounded to the nearest hundredth?**

F 1.4 meters

G 1.5 meters

H 1.47 meters

J 1.48 meters

45 **Shondra took her temperature with a Fahrenheit thermometer. Her temperature was 98.6°F. Approximately what was her temperature in degrees Celsius?**

A 0

B 12

C 37

D 1,000

46 **Minerva wrote the numbers 1 through 10 on ten index cards.**

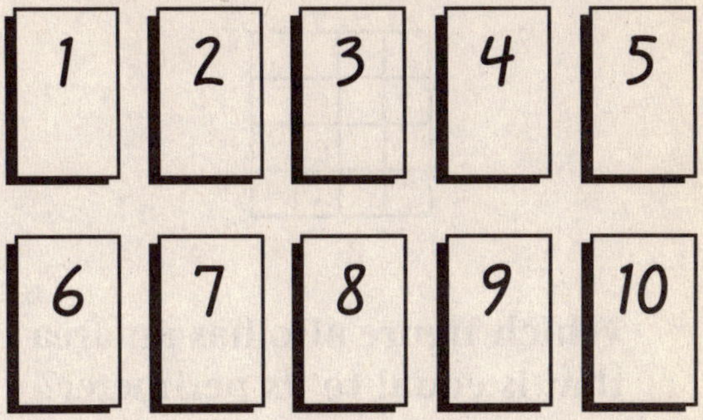

Which question about the cards could be answered using probability?

F How many piles of two cards could Minerva make using her index cards?

G What is the likelihood that Minerva will select the card marked with the number 8 if she chooses a card without looking?

H What is the sum of all the numbers Minerva wrote on her ten index cards?

J If Minerva continued to write numbers on more index cards, how many more would she need to have a stack of cards numbered 1 through 40?

Go to next page

47 This figure has an area of 16 and a perimeter of 16.

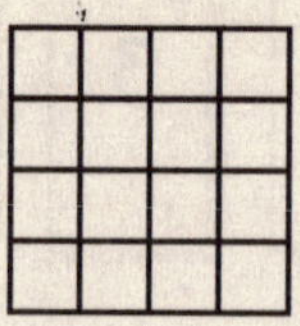

Which figure also has an area that is equal to its perimeter?

A 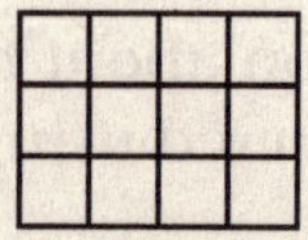

B 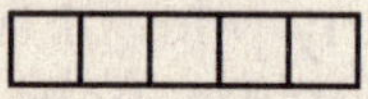

C 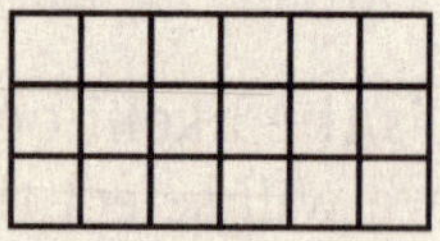

D 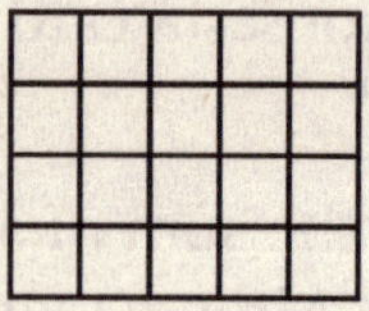

48 If $D = 8$, then $48 \div D =$

F 4

G 6

H 12

J 40

49 

What is the value of point *K* on the number line?

A 34

B 42

C 46

D 47

50 These four sums form a pattern.

$1 + 2 = 3$

$1 + 2 + 3 = 6$

$1 + 2 + 3 + 4 = 10$

$1 + 2 + 3 + 4 + 5 = 15$

What will be the *6th* sum in the pattern?

F 25

G 28

H 30

J 42

Go to next page

51 **Jim has y comic books. Suzy has five more comic books than Jim. Which expression tells how many comic books Suzy has?**

A $y + 5$

B $y - 5$

C $y \times 5$

D $y \div 5$

52 **Manuela's school day begins at 7:45 A.M. and ends at 2:25 P.M. How long is Manuela's school day?**

F 5 hours and 40 minutes

G 5 hours and 50 minutes

H 6 hours and 20 minutes

J 6 hours and 40 minutes

53 **The decimal model below represents what number?**

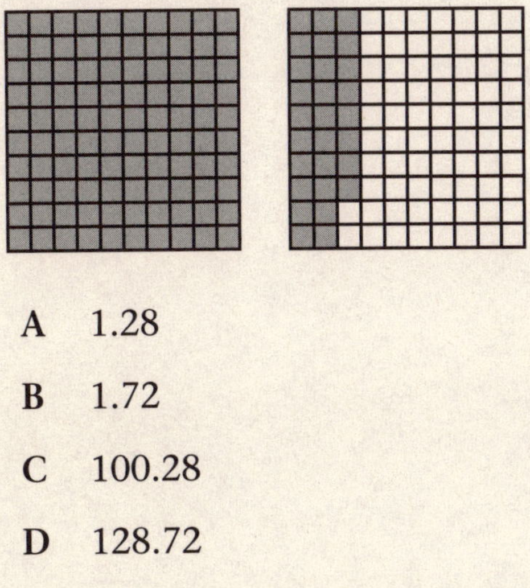

A 1.28

B 1.72

C 100.28

D 128.72

54

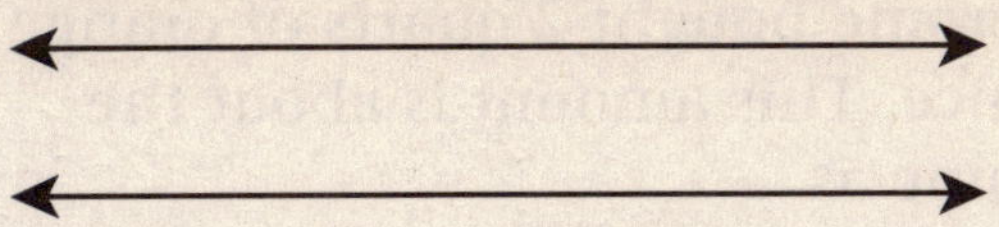

These two lines are best described as —

F rays

G perimeters

H perpendicular lines

J parallel lines

55 **Linda goes to a pet store. She wants to buy a dog, a parrot, a cat, and a snake. Linda's parents tell her that she can buy exactly two pets, but she can't buy two of the same pet. Which lists all the different possible combinations of two pets that Linda could buy?**

A dog and parrot; dog and cat; dog and snake; cat and snake

B dog and cat; snake and parrot; dog and parrot; cat and snake

C dog and parrot; dog and cat; dog and snake; parrot and cat; parrot and snake; cat and snake

D dog and parrot; dog and snake; cat and parrot; cat and snake; parrot and dog; parrot and cat; snake and cat; snake and dog

Go to next page

56 **Jerome bought 2 quarts of orange juice. This amount is about the same as —**

F 1 liter

G 2 liters

H 2 gallons

J 1 kiloliter

57 **Aretha rolled a six-sided number cube. Each of the sides of the cube is marked with one of the following numbers: 1, 2, 3, 4, 5, and 6. What is the probability that Aretha rolled an even number?**

A $\frac{3}{6}$

B $\frac{2}{6}$

C $\frac{1}{6}$

D $\frac{6}{3}$

58 **Which value is missing from this pattern?**

42, 35, 28, ____, 14

F 7

G 15

H 21

J 27

59 **Which statement is correct?**

A 8,900,406 < 8,875,825

B 8,561,072 < 8,486,917

C 8,145,333 < 8,080,085

D 8,864,924 < 8,871,302

60 **Study this pattern formed by letters.**

a b C d e F g h I j

What will the 12th letter look like if the pattern continues?

F **m**

G **k**

H **l**

J **L**

STOP

Answer Key for Miles

Mile 1

E 1. 7,405,634 is greater than 7,398,113, so you should have circled 7,405,634.

L 2. 1,134,509 is greater than 1,132,798, so you should have drawn a square around 1,134,509.

V 3. 4,560,001 and four million five hundred sixty thousand and one are the same, so you should have drawn a star around the second number, 4,506,001.

I 4. 5,498,102 is greater than 5,468,376, so you should have drawn a diamond around 5,498,102.

S 5. Seven million, two hundred fifty three thousand and two (or 7,253,002) is greater than 7,235,002, so you should have drawn an "X" through seven million, two hundred fifty three thousand and two.

Elvis is the famous rock star.

---

1. B
2. H
3. A
4. G
5. D

Mile 2

1. G
2. A
3. R
4. F
5. I
6. E
7. L
8. D

Garfield is the last name of the twentieth U.S. president and a popular cartoon character.

---

1. D
2. J
3. A
4. H
5. D

Mile 3

Mercury	35,991,000 → 36,000,000
Venus	67,246,000 → 67,200,000
Earth	92,956,000 → 93,000,000
Mars	141,665,000 → 141,700,000
Jupiter	483,732,000 → 483,700,000
Saturn	886,843,000 → 886,800,000
Uranus	1,784,320,000 → 1,784,300,000
Neptune	2,794,929,000 → 2,794,900,000
Pluto	3,675,253,000 → 3,675,300,000

1. A
2. J
3. B
4. G
5. A

Mile 4

[1] 4	6	[2] 5			
2		3			
[3] 7	8	4	[4] 1		
8			6		
		[5] 2	5	[6] 4	
		7		9	
		[7] 8	0	9	0
[8] 7	7	8			

1. C
2. J
3. B
4. F
5. D

Mile 5

1. I → 162
2. S → 3,220
3. A → 19,671
4. A → 4,375
5. C → 693
6. N → 52,592
7. E → 10,488
8. W → 141
9. T → 35,746
10. O → 1,445
11. N → 236,551

The famous mathematician is **Isaac Newton.**

---

1. C
2. F
3. D
4. J
5. A
6. G

Mile 6

1. 31 R3
2. 107 R4
3. 12 R2
4. 68 R0
5. 64 R1
6. 8 R7
7. 69 R6
8. 18 R10
9. 12 R11
10. 42 R5
11. 502 R13
12. 6 R8
13. 13 R9

The singer is **Britney Spears.**

---

1. C
2. G
3. B
4. H
5. B

Mile 7

1. 42 cookies
2. 3 slices
3. $10.00
4. $1.40
5. $1.50

---

1. C
2. G
3. B
4. J

Mile 8

1. $\begin{array}{r} 30 \\ \times\ 10 \\ \hline 300 \end{array}$
2. $\begin{array}{r} 90 \\ \times\ 10 \\ \hline 900 \end{array}$
3. $\begin{array}{r} 50 \\ \times\ 50 \\ \hline 2{,}500 \end{array}$
4. $\begin{array}{r} 140 \\ \times\ 70 \\ \hline 9{,}800 \end{array}$
5. $\begin{array}{r} 240 \\ \times\ 20 \\ \hline 4{,}800 \end{array}$
6. $10\overline{)40} = 4$
7. $10\overline{)90} = 9$
8. $20\overline{)120} = 6$
9. $60\overline{)180} = 3$
10. $70\overline{)140} = 2$

Here are the remaining numbers ordered from greatest to least:

G → 700

O → 550

L → 490

D → 420

I → 380

L → 240

O → 110

C → 89

K → 50

S → 10

The answer to the riddle is **Goldilocks.**

---

1. C
2. J
3. D
4. F

Mile 9

1. S
2. I
3. M
4. P
5. S
6. O
7. N

► The last name of the popular television family is **Simpson**.

---

1. C
2. F
3. D
4. G

Mile 10

Scales 1, 4, 6, and 7 are tilted incorrectly, so you should have marked an "X" on each one.

Scales 2, 3, 5, 8, 9, and 10 are tilted correctly, so you should have circled each one.

---

1. A
2. H
3. C
4. G
5. D

Mile 11

Chicken	3.22 lb.	→	3.2 lb.
	$4.09	→	$4.10
Hamburgers	2.48 lb.	→	2.5 lb.
	$4.63	→	$4.60
Potatoes	9.83 lb.	→	9.8 lb.
	$3.84	→	$3.80
Carrots	4.27 lb.	→	4.3 lb.
	$4.17	→	$4.20
Tomatoes	3.36 lb.	→	3.4 lb.
	$3.49	→	$3.50

1. $20.20
2. 23.2 lb.

---

1. C
2. F
3. B
4. G
5. D

Mile 12

1. J = 0.424
2. C = 34.86
3. O = 12.26
4. M = 6.86
5. R = 75.1
6. I = 14.01
7. D = 23.90
8. H = 0.890
9. E = 73.1
10. A = 0.98
11. N = 21
12. L = 16.001
13. A = 60.968

The famous basketball star is **Michael Jordan.**

---

1. D
2. F
3. D
4. F

Mile 13

1. 30.24 → READ
2. 2 → A
3. 5.116 → BOOK
4. 2.84 → AND
5. 9.0238 → LEARN

The secret message is **Read a book and learn.**

---

1. D
2. H
3. B
4. J
5. C

Mile 14

1. B
2. C
3. A
4. E
5. D

---

1. B
2. H
3. D

Mile 15

1. LaTanya
2. $\frac{1}{4}$
3. $\frac{6}{8}$
4. $\frac{3}{4}$

---

1. A
2. G
3. B
4. F
5. B

Mile 16

I $\frac{1}{3}$ $\frac{3}{9}$	V [illegible]	N $\frac{2}{5}$ $\frac{4}{10}$	Y [illegible]	A [illegible]
C [illegible]	H $\frac{1}{2}$ $\frac{3}{6}$	R [illegible]	I $\frac{3}{4}$ $\frac{9}{12}$	S $\frac{1}{3}$ $\frac{2}{6}$
B [illegible]	D [illegible]	S $\frac{2}{3}$ $\frac{4}{6}$	O [illegible]	L $\frac{1}{5}$ $\frac{2}{10}$
W [illegible]	E $\frac{1}{6}$ $\frac{2}{12}$	E $\frac{1}{4}$ $\frac{2}{8}$	K [illegible]	V $\frac{1}{2}$ $\frac{6}{12}$
I $\frac{4}{5}$ $\frac{8}{10}$	N [illegible]	E $\frac{1}{4}$ $\frac{2}{8}$	S $\frac{1}{4}$ $\frac{3}{12}$	D [illegible]

The general kept his armies **in his sleevies.**

---

1. C
2. G

Mile 17

1. G → $\frac{2}{9}$
2. R → $\frac{3}{3} = 1$
3. O → $\frac{4}{19}$
4. V → $\frac{5}{7}$
5. E → $\frac{4}{21}$
6. R → $\frac{13}{19}$
7. C → 0
8. L → $3\frac{7}{8}$
9. E → $\frac{5}{21}$
10. V → $\frac{6}{8} = \frac{3}{4}$
11. E → $\frac{5}{29}$
12. L → $\frac{6}{14} = \frac{3}{7}$
13. A → $7\frac{4}{9}$
14. N → $\frac{1}{3}$
15. D → $\frac{8}{10} = \frac{4}{5}$

The 22nd and 24th U.S. president was **Grover Cleveland.**

---

1. C
2. G
3. D
4. H

Mile 18

1. D
2. A
3. B
4. F
5. E
6. C
7. $\frac{33}{100} = 0.33$
8. $\frac{4}{10} = 0.4$
9. Julie finished the homework faster. $\frac{4}{5}$ of an hour = 0.80 of an hour. 0.85 is greater than 0.80, so you know that Armando took more time to complete the homework.

---

1. A
2. G
3. B
4. H

Mile 19

1. 26 centimeters
2. 20 inches
3. 32 centimeters
4. 41 centimeters
5. 12 inches

A **crane** is the type of bird that can lift the most.

---

1. D
2. F
3. B

Mile 20

1. 45 feet^2
2. 72 feet^2
3. 400 inches^2

---

1. C
2. G
3. D
4. J

Mile 21

1. Perimeter = 12; Area = 8 → A S
2. Perimeter = 14; Area = 12 → P A
3. Perimeter = 14; Area = 10 → P U
4. Perimeter = 22; Area = 24 → L C
5. Perimeter = 18; Area = 18 → E E

The name of the delicious food revealed by the activity is **apple sauce.**

---

1. A
2. H
3. B
4. F

Mile 22

1. diameter
2. the center
3. chord
4. radius

---

1. B
2. J
3. C
4. G

Mile 23

1. Line; the letter i and n should be circled.
2. Perpendicular; the letters d and i should be circled.
3. Ray; the letter a should be circled.
4. Segment; the letter s should be circled.
5. Point; the letter p should be circled.
6. Parallel; the first letter a should be circled.
7. Intersect; the letters i and n should be circled.

Country #1: India

Country #2: Spain

---

1. B
2. H
3. B

Mile 24

1. obtuse, 135°
2. acute, 50°
3. right, 90°
4. obtuse, 110°

---

1. B
2. F
3. A
4. H

Mile 25

1. $\angle C = 80°$
2. $\angle G = 60°$
3. $\angle I = 45°$
4. $\angle R = 35°$

---

1. B
2. G
3. D
4. G

Mile 26

(5, 5)	(5, 3)	(7, 3)		(3, 9)	(7, 7)	(3, 7)	(3, 7)	(9, 9)	(5, 3)		(7, 3)
M	R	S	.	B	I	G	G	E	R	'	S

(3, 9)	(1, 9)	(3, 9)	(7, 1)		(7, 7)	(7, 3)		(1, 9)
B	A	B	Y		I	S		A

(3, 5)	(7, 7)	(9, 3)	(9, 3)	(3, 5)	(9, 9)		(3, 9)	(7, 7)	(3, 7)	(3, 7)	(9, 9)	(5, 3)
L	I	T	T	L	E		B	I	G	G	E	R

---

1. C
2. F
3. C

Mile 27

1. tons
2. square kilometers
3. milliliters
4. meters
5. gallons
6. miles
7. grams
8. inches

---

1. D
2. G
3. D

Mile 28

1. B → 3
2. H → 150
3. E → 15
4. U → 70
5. D → 2
6. Y → 500
7. A → 96
8. T → 8
9. C → 82
10. L → 320

320	15	8	8	70	82	15
L	E	T	T	U	C	E

,

3	500
B	Y

96
A

150	15	96	2
H	E	A	D

---

1. C
2. F
3. C
4. G

Mile 29

64-oz. dumbbell → 4-lb. bowling pin

12-lb. bowling ball → 192-oz. potted plant

1-ton car → 2,000-lb. Liberty Bell

4,000-kg elephant → 4-metric-ton sailboat

---

1. C
2. J
3. A
4. G

Mile 30

1. Quarts; the letter q should be circled.
2. Ounces; the letter u should be circled.
3. Gallons; the letter a should be circled.
4. Cups; the letter c should be circled.
5. Kiloliters; the letter k should be circled.
6. Liters; the letter e should be circled.
7. Milliliters; the letter r should be circled.
8. Pints; the letter s should be circled.

The answer to the riddle is **quackers.**

---

1. A
2. G
3. D
4. H
5. C

Mile 31

1. D; hot summer day (95°F) → 35°C
2. B; cold winter day (2°C) → 36°F
3. A; hot day in the desert (120°F) → 49°C
4. E; mild spring day (20°C) → 68°F
5. C; boiling water (100°C) → 212°F

---

1. C
2. G
3. A
4. F

Mile 32

You should have crossed out the first row (B), fourth row (C), sixth row (K), ninth row (N), and eleventh row (D).

The answer to the riddle is **lawsuit.**

---

1. B
2. J
3. D
4. H
5. A

Mile 33

1. 30 → M
2. 2 → S
3. 100 → O

The answer to the riddle is **missile toe.**

---

1. D
2. G
3. A
4. J

Mile 34

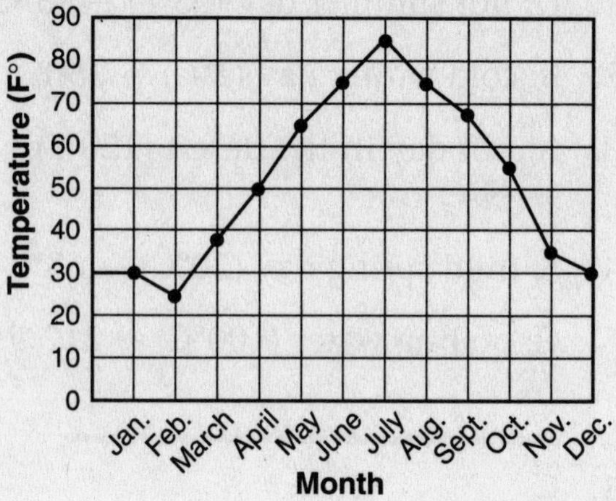

1. July is the hottest month of the year. February is the coldest month of the year.
2. April and May
3. October and November

---

1. C
2. F

Mile 35

Stem	Leaf
2	0,1,4,4,8
3	0,2,2,2,5,6,6
4	1,4,5,7
5	3
6	0,1,1,5,9

The answer to the riddle is **banner day.**

1. A
2. H

Mile 36

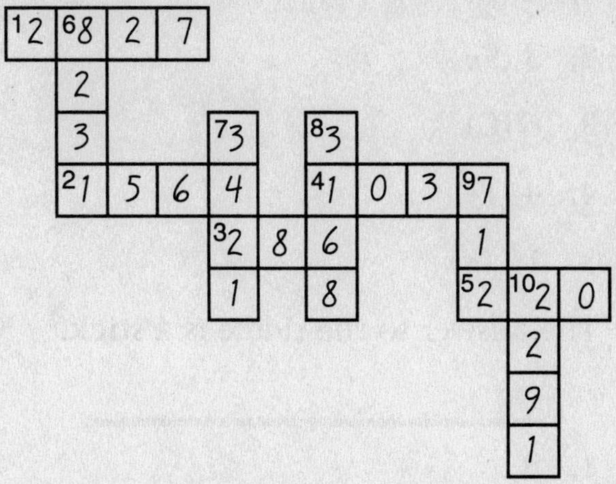

1. B
2. G
3. B

Mile 37

1. 5 (I)
2. 3 (S)
3. 6 (C)
4. 4 (T)
5. 10 (K)

The answer to the riddle is a **stick.**

---

1. B
2. J
3. A
4. J

Mile 38

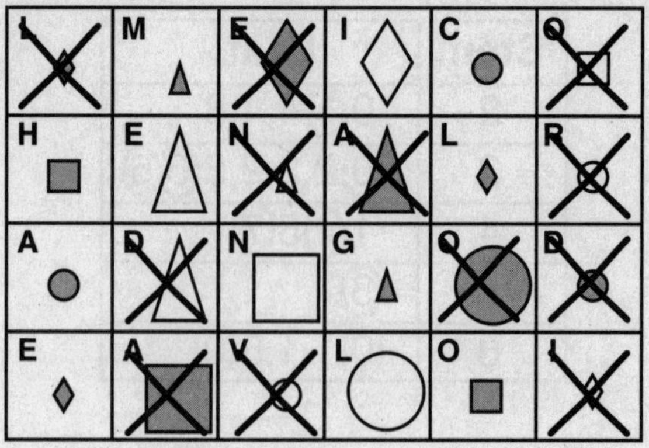

The name of the famous artist is **Michelangelo.**

---

1. D
2. G

Mile 39

1. 8
2. 16
3. 12
4. 44
5. 11
6. 12
7. 30
8. 20
9. 8
10. 49

The famous American inventor is **Eli Whitney.**

---

1. A
2. G
3. B
4. J
5. A

Mile 40

Possible combinations:

pizza with no toppings
pizza with sausage
pizza with peppers
pizza with extra cheese
pizza with sausage and peppers
pizza with sausage and extra cheese
pizza with peppers and extra cheese
pizza with sausage, peppers, and extra cheese

There are 8 possible combinations for you to choose from.

---

1. B
2. H

Mile 41

1. C $\frac{1}{8}$
2. H $\frac{3}{8}$
3. E $\frac{2}{8}$
4. W $\frac{5}{8}$
5. S $\frac{4}{8}$
6. D $\frac{7}{8}$
7. A $\frac{8}{8}$
8. Y $\frac{6}{8}$

Monsters eat on **Chewsday**!

---

1. C
2. G

Mile 42

Problems 1, 3, 6, 9, and 13 are not probability problems.

Problems 2, 4, 5, 7, 8, 10, 11, 12, 14, and 15 are probability problems.

The second largest city in Egypt is **Alexandria.**

---

1. B
2. J

Mile 43

1. 14 → P
2. 25 → O
3. 4 → R
4. 18 → K
5. 6 → Y
6. 19 → P
7. 5 → I
8. 99 → G

The famous cartoon character is **Porky Pig!**

---

1. A
2. G
3. C
4. J
5. D

Mile 44

1. E; five more than a number → $5 + x$
2. C; three times a number → $3 \times a$
3. O; six less than a number → $z - 6$
4. K; a number divided by eight → $b \div 8$
5. F; seven times a number → $7 \times f$
6. A; double a number → $2 \times q$
7. H; four less than a number → $y - 4$
8. I; nine divided by a number → $9 \div p$
9. Q; one less than a number → $x - 1$
10. L; four divided by a number → $4 \div m$
11. S; four times a number → $4 \times k$
12. D; two divided by a number → $2 \div y$
13. M; eight more than a number → $b + 8$
14. N; a number divided by five → $x \div 5$
15. G; six times a number → $6 \times d$
16. T; a number divided by two → $s \div 2$
17. J; one more than a number → $h + 1$
18. R; two more than a number → $b + 2$
19. B; seven less than a number → $w - 7$
20. P; nine times a number → $x \times 9$

---

1. A
2. J
3. C
4. H
5. D

Mile 45

1. $W \times 2 = 20$
2. $M = 7 + 1$
3. $C = 20 \times 2$
4. $Y = 82 + 5$
5. $Z + 270 = 640$

---

1. D
2. F
3. B

Answers and Explanations for Practice Test 1

Answer Key for Practice Test 1

Section 1

1. C
2. G
3. B
4. J
5. B
6. J
7. C
8. F
9. C
10. J
11. B
12. H
13. C
14. H

Section 2

15. C
16. F
17. D
18. J
19. C
20. J
21. D
22. H
23. B
24. F
25. B
26. G
27. A
28. G

29. B
30. F
31. D
32. F
33. A
34. J
35. C
36. H
37. A
38. H
39. D
40. F
41. C
42. H
43. B
44. F
45. D
46. H
47. B
48. J
49. B
50. H
51. A
52. F
53. D
54. G
55. C
56. H
57. B
58. J
59. D
60. F

Answers and Explanations for Practice Test 1

Section 1

1. **C** To calculate the contribution of each businessperson, you must divide the total amount of money contributed by the number of businesspeople who contributed. 6,372 ÷ 36 = 177, so each businessperson contributed $177.00. If you chose answer choice **A**, you subtracted when you were supposed to divide. If you chose answer choice **D**, you misplaced the decimal point. You could have avoided this mistake by setting up the problem as $36\overline{)6{,}372}$.

2. **G** It is usually best to rewrite this type of problem so that the numbers are stacked one on top of another. Rewrite the problem this way.

$$\begin{array}{r} 0.4 \\ \times\ 8.3 \\ \hline \end{array}$$

Then multiply as you would two whole numbers. When you are done, count the total number of decimal places in the two numbers you are multiplying and place the decimal point that many places to the left in your product. In this case each number has one decimal place, which makes two places total. The product of 0.4 and 8.3 is 3.32. That's answer choice **G**.

3. **B** You can solve this problem by rounding each number to the nearest thousand. 13,321 rounded to the nearest thousand is 13,000. 6,658 rounded to the nearest thousand is 7,000. 13,000 + 7,000 = 20,000, which is the correct answer to this question.

4. **J** Because both fractions have the same denominator, all you have to do is add the numerators and reduce the result. $\frac{1}{8} + \frac{5}{8} = \frac{6}{8}$. $\frac{6}{8}$ reduces to $\frac{3}{4}$.

5. **B** To determine the amount of change Andrea should have received, subtract the cost of the calculator from $20, the amount of money she gave the sales clerk. 20.00 – 14.82 = 5.18. If you chose answer choices **A** or **D**, you probably did not borrow numbers correctly when you subtracted. You can practice addition and subtraction by completing Mile 4.

6. **J** Good news: because $\frac{3}{8}$ is less than $\frac{7}{8}$, you don't have to borrow to solve this subtraction problem. And because the two fractions have the same denominator, all you have to do is subtract the numerators. $\frac{7}{8} - \frac{3}{8} = \frac{4}{8}$; $8 - 2 = 6$. Therefore, $8\frac{7}{8} - 2\frac{3}{8} = 6\frac{4}{8}$, which reduces to $6\frac{1}{2}$.

7. **C** Be careful when calculating in order to avoid making careless mistakes. Answer choice **A**, 156, is 52 + 104. You get this result by failing to align numbers properly before adding. Answer choice **B** is the result of failing to carry numbers properly. If you made either of these mistakes, slow down on multiplication problems. Slowing down should help you reduce the number of careless errors you make.

8. **F** To answer this question, you must first determine the value of each tick mark on the number line. This number line is divided into units of 20. Write 220, 240, 260, and 280 under the tick marks between 200 and 300, and you will see that this is so. The point shown on the number line is between 240 and 260. That means it is approximately 250. Now check each answer choice to find the one that is closest to 250. Answer choice **F**, 504 ÷ 2, equals 252. None of the other answers is this close to 250, so **F** is the correct answer.

9. **C** It is usually best to rewrite this type of problem so that the numbers are stacked one on top of another. Rewrite the problem as

$$\begin{array}{r} 3.6 \\ \underline{\times\ 7.2} \end{array}$$

Then multiply as you would two whole numbers. When you are done, count the total number of decimal places in the two numbers you are multiplying and place the decimal point that many places to the left in your product. In this case each number has one decimal place, which makes two places total. The product of 3.6 and 7.2 is 25.92.

10. **J** First, determine how much money Milo has left over after he pays for the asparagus. Asparagus costs $2.80 per pound, so that leaves Milo with $2.20. Three pounds of onions (answer choice **A**) cost 3 × $0.99 = $2.97, so Milo does not have enough money to buy 3 pounds of onions. Cross off answer choice **A.** Four pounds of peppers (answer choice **B**) cost 4 × $0.85 = $3.40, so Milo does not have enough money to buy 4 pounds of peppers. Cross off answer choice **B.** One pound of potatoes, 1 pound of onions, and 1 pound of peppers (answer choice **C**) cost $0.45 + $0.99 + $0.85 = $2.29, so Milo does not have enough money to buy these items. Cross off answer choice **C.** He does have enough money to buy 3 pounds of potatoes (3 × $0.45 = $1.35) and 1 pound of peppers, because $1.35 + $0.85 = $2.20. That makes **D** the correct answer choice.

11. **B** It is easier to solve division problems if you put the number to be divided inside the division sign and then divide. Rewrite this problem as $12\overline{)2{,}940}$

    Then divide. The result is 245. There is no remainder. If you had trouble with this problem, review division by completing Mile 6.

12. **H** To add $\frac{5}{6}$ and $\frac{1}{3}$, you must find a common denominator for the two fractions. The common denominator is 6. Rewrite the fractions as $\frac{5}{6}$ and $\frac{2}{6}$ and then add to get $\frac{7}{6}$. Convert $\frac{7}{6}$ to the mixed number $1\frac{1}{6}$.

13. **C** When the dividend is a decimal, put a decimal in the quotient right above the decimal in the dividend. Do this first so you don't forget! Then divide as you would two whole numbers. If you did not come up with the answer 0.238, you probably put the decimal point in the wrong place. You should review division with decimals by completing Mile 13.

14. **H** To find out how many crates Phil needs to hold his 192 jars of jam, divide 192 by 24, the number of jars each crate can hold. If you divide correctly, you will come up with 8. Answer choice **F** is the product of 192 and 24; answer choice **G** is the sum of 192 and 24. If you chose either of these incorrect answer choices, you probably made a careless mistake. Slow down when you take the test so you can avoid making careless errors.

15. **C** To compare decimals, you must compare similar decimal places in each number, moving left to right from the decimal point. Compare the tenths places first, then the hundredths, then the thousandths, and so on. You only have to compare until you find a pair of digits that are not the same. If the tenths digits are not equal, for example, you do not need to compare the hundredths or thousandths digits. Simply compare the tenths digits and you are done. The decimal with the greater tenths digit has the greater value. If a number stops before you have finished comparing, simply attach zeros until both numbers have the same number of places after the decimal point. To compare the decimals in answer choice **A**, for example, attach a 0 to 0.4 to make it 0.40. Now it is easier to see that 0.45 is greater than 0.40. In the correct answer you need only compare values to the hundredths place. Since 3 is greater than 1, 0.53 is greater than 0.5187.

16. **F** There are two white marbles in the bag. There are nine marbles in total in the bag. Therefore, the chances that Raya will select a white marble from the bag are 2 in 9, or $\frac{2}{9}$. Review Mile 41 if you feel you need more of a review on probability.

17. **D** In the first group six out of eight sheep, or $\frac{6}{8}$ of the sheep, are white. Three out of four sheep, or $\frac{3}{4}$ of the sheep, in answer choice **D** are white. Reduce $\frac{6}{8}$ by dividing the numerator and denominator by 2 to determine that $\frac{6}{8}$ and $\frac{3}{4}$ are equal.

18. **J** To find the mean of a set of numbers, add the numbers together. Then divide by however many numbers are in the set. In this problem there are six numbers in the set. The sum of the six numbers is 56 + 64 + 58 + 66 + 66 + 56 = 366. Divide 366 by 6 to find the correct answer, which is 61. Don't forget that you are allowed to use your calculator on this part of the test! Review Mile 36 if you feel you need more work on averages.

19. **C** Look at the triangles to try and find a pattern. Triangle 2 uses 3 more dots than Triangle 1 uses. Triangle 3 uses 4 more dots than Triangle 2 uses. How many more dots will Triangle 4 use? The pattern is 3, 4, ... Did you guess that the next number is 5? If you did, you are correct. Triangle 4 will have 5 dots more than Triangle 3. Triangle 3 has 10 dots, so Triangle 4 will have 15 dots.

20. **J** The decimal model is divided into one hundred equal squares. Therefore, the decimal model represents a decimal that extends to the hundredths place. Fifty-three squares are shaded, meaning that the decimal model represents $\frac{53}{100}$, which is written in decimal form as 0.53. Because the decimal model represents a number with a value less than 1, you could have used POE to eliminate every answer choice except the correct one!

21. **D** To find the area of a square, multiply the length of a side of the square by itself. $6 \times 6 = 36$, so the area of the square is 36 feet^2. If you chose answer choice C, 24 feet^2, you were probably thinking of perimeter instead of area. Remember, area is measured in square units; perimeter is not.

22. **H** According to the bar graph Bill Henderson received thirty votes, Amelia Rodriguez received forty votes, Nancy Schwartz received twenty-five votes, and Vernon King received thirty-five votes. If this is unclear to you, you should review bar graphs by rereading Mile 33.

23. **B** To answer this question, you must remember that the ten-thousandths place in a decimal is four places to the right of the decimal point. Because you are looking for a decimal that equals "seven and one hundred fifty-three ten-thousandths," you must find an answer that extends exactly four places to the right of the decimal point. Only answer choice **B** does this. Therefore, you can use POE to get rid of answers choices **A**, **C**, and **D**.

24. **F** Study the numbers in the right-hand column of the table until you determine a pattern. You should notice that each number is exactly 0.75 more than the number before it. To continue the pattern, continue adding 0.75. A stairway with nine steps will be 6.75 feet tall; a stairway with ten steps will be 7.5 feet tall.

25. **B** A meter is slightly more than 3 feet long. Therefore, Charles is slightly more than 6 feet tall. You can review approximate comparisons of metric and U.S. customary lengths by completing Mile 28.

26. **G** Compare each answer choice to $\frac{1}{2}$. You can compare fractions by using the bowtie method. Multiply the denominator of each fraction by the numerator of the other. Write the products by the numerators. The fraction with the larger number by the numerator is the larger fraction. Review the cross-multiplication method by completing Mile 16. Here's another tip that helps with this problem. You can easily determine whether a fraction is greater than or less than $\frac{1}{2}$ by doubling the numerator. If the result is greater than the denominator, then the fraction is greater than $\frac{1}{2}$. If the result is less than the denominator, then the fraction is less than $\frac{1}{2}$. If the result equals the denominator, then the fraction equals $\frac{1}{2}$.

27. **A** The lengths of the sides of the triangle are 4 centimeters, 6 centimeters, and 7 centimeters. (If you did not come up with these results, you need to practice measuring lines with your centimeter ruler.) The perimeter of a triangle is the sum of the lengths of its sides, so the perimeter of this triangle is 4 + 6 + 7, or 17 centimeters.

28. **G** Area tells you how much space an item takes up. You would need to know how much space a floor takes up in order to cover it completely with carpet. To fill a swimming pool (answer choice **F**), you would need to know the volume of the pool. To enclose a yard with fencing (answer choice **H**) or wrap ribbon around a package (answer choice **J**), you would need to know the perimeter of the yard or the package.

29. **B** There are two rules for the pattern shown in this question. The first rule involves the shapes, which go "moon, lightning bolt, moon, lightning bolt…," The second rule has to do with whether the shapes are right side up or upside down. The first three shapes in the pattern are right side up, while the next three shapes in the pattern are upside down. Shapes 7, 8, and 9, then, will be right side up. Because shape 6 is a lightning bolt, shape 7 will be a right side up moon.

30. **F** To round a decimal to the nearest tenth, look at the digit in the hundredths place. If the digit is 0, 1, 2, 3, or 4, eliminate the digit and every digit to its right. If the digit is 5, 6, 7, 8, or 9, add 1 to the tenths digit. Then eliminate the hundredths digit and every digit to its right. Because the hundredths digit in 7.18 is 8, you should add 1 to the tenths digit and get rid of all digits to the right. The result is 7.2.

31. **D** Because distance must be measured in a unit of length, you can eliminate answer choice **C** which is a measure of volume. Because the distance from California to Virginia is very far, you would want to use a large unit to measure the distance. Think of how big the number of inches from California to Virginia would be! That is why "miles" is the best answer.

32. **F** The best way to answer this problem is by using POE. Answer choices **G, H,** and **J** present questions that can be answered simply by counting; you do not need to calculate probability to answer any of them. Because probability is used to calculate the likelihood that something will happen, it would be useful to figure out how likely a result a roll of 7 on two number cubes is. Review Mile 42 if you want to work on more probability problems.

33. **A** Here is an easy way to solve this type of problem. First, count how many minutes elapse from the starting time until the beginning of the hour. Then, count the number of complete hours that elapse between the beginning of the hour and the ending time. Finally, count the number of minutes that elapse from the beginning of the hour until the ending time. In this problem there are 45 minutes from the starting time of 11:15 A.M. to the beginning of the hour. There are no complete hours between 12:00 P.M. and 12:40 P.M. There are 40 minutes between 12:00 P.M. and 12:40 P.M. Therefore, 45 + 40 = 85 minutes. If you subtract 60 minutes (which equals 1 hour) from that, you get 1 hour and 25 minutes. That's answer choice **A**.

34. **J** The radius of a circle is a line segment drawn from the center of the circle to a point on the outside of the circle. *XE* is a radius of the circle. *AB* and *DE* are chords; *CD* is a diameter.

35. **C** To compare six-digit numbers, look at corresponding digits from left to right. Start with the hundred-thousands digits. If they are not equal, your work is done. Whichever number has the greater hundred-thousands digit is the greater number. If the digits are equal, compare the ten-thousands digit, the thousands digit, and so on until you find a pair of digits that are not equal. To confirm that answer choice **C** is correct, you must compare the hundreds digit. Because 5 is greater than 1, 564,535 is greater than 564,107.

36. **H** A right triangle is a triangle that, by definition, has one right corner. Right corners measure 90°. It is impossible for a triangle to have more than one 90° angle (answer choice **J**). A right triangle may have two equal angles (answer choice **F**)—when it does it is called a right isosceles triangle—but it does not have to have two equal sides. A triangle with three equal sides (answer choice **G**) is called an equilateral triangle. All three of its angles measure 60°.

37. **A** To determine how to divide a large group into smaller teams, you must use the operation of division. Because only answer choice **A** includes division, you can use POE to get rid of all the incorrect answer choices.

38. **H** Because Chet tosses the coin twice, the diagram showing all the possible results must have two columns. Knowing this allows you to eliminate answer choices **F** and **J**. Answer choice **G** correctly shows that "heads" and "tails" are the only possible results of the first toss; however, it does not show all the possible results of the second toss. It does not show "heads-heads" or "tails-tails." Therefore, you can eliminate answer choice **G**. That leaves only answer choice **H**, which correctly shows all the possible results of the two coin tosses.

39. **D** Remember, the mode is the number that appears the most often in a group of numbers. What number appears most often among Mollie's bowling scores? That number is 162, which appears three times in the group of numbers.

40. **F** To answer this question, you must remember that the hundredths place in a decimal is two places to the right of the decimal point. Because you are looking for a decimal that equals "twelve and five one-hundredths," you must find an answer choice that extends exactly two places to the right of the decimal point. Only answer choice **F** does this. Therefore, you can use POE to get rid of answer choices **G**, **H**, and **J**. Review Mile 9 if you want to practice recognizing decimal places some more.

41. **C** Put your finger on 1991 at the bottom of the graph. Then run your finger straight up until you touch the line showing the population of Virginia. Keep your finger on the line and then look at the numbers running up the left margin of the graph. Where is your finger in relation to the numbers? If you've done everything correctly, your finger should be between 6,200,000 and 6,400,000. That means the population of Virginia was between those two numbers in 1991. Only answer choice **C**, 6,300,000, is between 6,200,000 and 6,400,000, so it has to be the correct answer.

42. **H** To answer this question, you must determine the value of each tick mark on the number line. Subtract a marked number represented on the number line from the number to its right. You will get a difference of 20. If you count the number of marks between each marked number, you get four. If you divide 20 by 4, you get 5, so each tick mark represents five numbers. Point T, which is one tick mark to the right of 70, has a value of 70 + 5, or 75.

43. **B** The best way to answer this question is to substitute 8 for X in each answer choice. $40 \div 8 = 5$, so **B** is the correct answer. If you chose answer choices **C** or **D**, you probably made a careless mistake. If you chose answer choice **C**, you mistook the minus sign in the answer for a division sign. If you chose answer choice **D**, you subtracted 5 from 8 instead of adding the two numbers. Slow down when you take the test to avoid making careless errors.

44. **F** Four of sixteen squares in the original figure are shaded. Therefore, $\frac{4}{16}$ of the figure is shaded. That means $\frac{1}{4}$ of the figure is shaded. The figure shown in answer choice **F** is also $\frac{1}{4}$ shaded, so **F** is the correct answer.

45. **D** You can use POE to answer this question. The correct answer must include the number 71 twice, because the stem-and-leaf plot lists 71 twice. Only one answer choice, **D**, lists 71 twice. Therefore, you can get rid of all the incorrect answer choices. If you need to review stem-and-leaf plots, go back to Mile 35.

46. **H** The lengths of the lines that form the W are 2.5 centimeters long, 1.5 centimeters long, 1.5 centimeters long, and 2.5 centimeters long. The sum of those four values is 2.5 + 1.5 + 1.5 + 2.5 = 8. The correct answer is 8 centimeters. If you did not come up with this result, you may need to practice measuring lines with your centimeter ruler.

47. **B** The pattern repeats every three shapes. In this pattern the first shape is the same as the 4th, the 2nd is the same as the 5th, and the 3rd is the same as the 6th. The 7th shape will be the same as the 1st and the 8th shape will be the same as the 2nd. Answer choice **B** shows the 2nd shape, so it is the correct answer.

48. **J** The figure is a rectangle with sides of 5 and 6. The area of a rectangle is calculated by multiplying the lengths of its sides, so the area of this rectangle is 30. The perimeter of a rectangle is the sum of its sides: 5 + 6 + 5 + 6 = 22.

49. **B** Andrea ran fifteen laps each day for seven days, so she ran a total of 15×7 laps.

50. **H** An acute angle is one that measures less than 90°. Only answer choice **H** shows an angle that measures less than 90°. The angle in answer choice **F** measures 180°. The angle in answer choice **G** is an obtuse angle, one that measures between 90° and 180°. The angle in answer choice **J** is a right corner that measures exactly 90°.

51. **A** A gallon equals 4 quarts, and a quart is only a little bit less than a liter. Therefore, a gallon of gasoline is closest to 4 liters. You can review approximate comparisons of metric liquid measures and U.S. customary liquid measures by completing Mile 30.

52. **F** This is a tricky question. This pattern is actually made up of two patterns. One pattern is formed by the 1st, 3rd, and 5th numbers: each is twice as large as the one before it (6, 12, 24, ...). The other pattern is formed by the 2nd, 4th, and 6th numbers in the pattern. They, too, are twice as large as the one before (9, 18, 36, ...). The 7th number in the pattern will be twice as large as the 5th number. The 5th number is 24, so the 7th number is 48.

53. **D** To find "*y* less than a number," you must subtract. If you realized this, you could get rid of all the incorrect answer choices. Review Mile 44 if you want to practice working on this type of question.

54. **G** The perimeter of a rectangle is the sum of its sides. 7 + 12 + 7 + 12 = 38. If you answered 19 (answer choice **F**), you forgot to add the lengths of all four sides of the rectangle. If you answered 84 (answer choice **J**), you calculated the area of the rectangle instead of its perimeter. Go back to Miles 19 and 20 to review the difference between area and perimeter.

55. **C** The spinner has eight spaces of equal size. Four of the spaces are black, so the chance that a spin will land on a black space are four out of eight, or $\frac{4}{8}$, which equals $\frac{1}{2}$.

56. **H** The open sentence $X \times 2 = ?$ involves multiplication. Which problem stated in the answer choices requires multiplication? You can answer this question using POE. Answer choice **F** asks a question that can be solved using addition. Answer choice **G** asks a question that can be solved using division. Answer choice **J** asks a question that can be solved using subtraction. Answer choice **H** can be solved by multiplying *X* by 2. This is the correct answer.

57. **B** There are three boys in a group of seven children, so boys make up $\frac{4}{7}$ of the group. Remember that a fraction expresses the relationship of a part to a whole, not a part to another part. That is why $\frac{4}{3}$, answer choice **D**, is not correct. It compares the number of boys to the number of girls. The correct answer must compare the number of boys to the entire group.

58. **J** The table shows that Donovan's weight increased every year. A graph of this data must show the same thing. Of the four graphs only the one in answer choice **J** shows Donovan's weight increasing every year. The graph in answer choice **H** shows his weight decreasing every year. The other answer choices show both increases and decreases and are incorrect.

59. **D** This question asks you to recognize a pattern in the soccer team's schedule. The rule of the pattern is the team plays a game, then it does not play for the next two days, then it plays again, then it does not play the next two days, and so on. The team played Game #4 on October 10, so it will play Game #5 on October 13 and Game #6 on October 16.

60. **F** The circumference of a circle is the distance around it. If you did not answer this question correctly, you should review circle terminology. Reread Mile 22 to learn about circles.

Answers and Explanations for Practice Test 2

Answer Key for Practice Test 2

Section 1

1. B
2. H
3. D
4. H
5. C
6. G
7. D
8. G
9. A
10. G
11. A
12. H
13. C
14. H

Section 2

15. C
16. J
17. C
18. H
19. D
20. G
21. D
22. H
23. B
24. G
25. A
26. J
27. A
28. G
29. C

30. H
31. A
32. H
33. C
34. H
35. B
36. J
37. B
38. J
39. D
40. H
41. C
42. G
43. A
44. J
45. C
46. G
47. C
48. G
49. B
50. G
51. A
52. J
53. A
54. J
55. C
56. G
57. A
58. H
59. D
60. J

Answers and Explanations for Practice Test 2

Section 1

1. **B** To answer this estimating problem, round the numbers to the nearest thousand. Round 49,036 to 49,000. Round 8,975 to 9,000. 49,000 – 9,000 = 40,000. The correct answer is **B**.

2. **H** 68,850 ÷ 25 = 274. If you had difficulty finding the answer to this question, you may need to practice long division. Complete Mile 6 to review division. If you made a careless mistake, make sure to slow down when you take the test.

3. **D** Multiply decimals as you would multiply two whole numbers. When you are done, count the total number of decimal places in the two numbers you are multiplying and place the decimal point that many places from the right in your product. In this case each number has one decimal place, which makes two places total. The product of 7.1 and 1.9 is 13.49.

4. **H** To add $\frac{3}{5}$ and $\frac{7}{10}$, you must find a common denominator for the two fractions. The common denominator is 10, so rewrite the fractions as $\frac{6}{10}$ and $\frac{7}{10}$. Then add to get $\frac{13}{10}$. Convert $\frac{13}{10}$ to the mixed number $1\frac{3}{10}$. If you chose answer choice **G**, you probably added the numerators and denominators without finding a common denominator first. Review addition with fractions by completing Mile 17.

5. **C** David has $20 to buy copies of a book that costs $5.25. Can he buy one copy? Yes, that would cost $5.25, and he has that much money. Can he buy two copies? Yes, two copies would cost $10.50, which is less than the $20 he has. How about three copies? Yes, three copies cost $15.75. Can he buy four copies? No. Four copies would cost $21.00, which is $1 more than he has. The greatest number of copies he can buy is three.

6. **G** It is usually best to rewrite this type of problem so that the numbers are stacked one on top of another. Rewrite the problem this way.

$$\begin{array}{r} 4{,}787 \\ \underline{+\ 2{,}432} \end{array}$$

Then add. Don't forget to carry or you may wind up with one of the incorrect answer choices. 4,787 + 2,432 = 7,219.

7. **D** The mittens cost $4.79 and the scarf costs $2.48. Together they cost $4.79 + $2.48 = $7.27. To find out how much change Melanie should have received, subtract $7.27 from $10.00. If you calculate correctly, you will arrive at the answer, $2.73.

8. **G** To find out how many boards will wind up in each of the piles, divide 364, the number of boards, by 28, the number of piles. If you divide correctly, you will come up with 13. If you chose answer choice **H**, you added instead of divided. If you chose answer choice **J**, you multiplied instead of divided. If you chose either of those incorrect answer choices, you probably made a careless mistake. Slow down when you take the test so that you can avoid making careless errors.

9. **A** Because the two fractions have the same denominator, all you have to do is add the numerators and reduce the sum. $\frac{4}{12} + \frac{5}{12} = \frac{9}{12}$, which reduces to $\frac{3}{4}$. If you had trouble with this problem, review Mile 17.

10. **G** First, rewrite this problem in this format.

$$3\overline{)0.516}$$

Remember that when the dividend is a decimal, you must make sure to put a decimal in the quotient right above the decimal in the dividend. Do this first so you don't forget! You should end up with the result shown below.

$$\begin{array}{r} 0.172 \\ 3\overline{)0.516} \\ \underline{-\ 3} \\ 21 \\ \underline{-\ 21} \\ 06 \\ \underline{-\ 6} \\ 0 \end{array}$$

11. **A** First, figure out the range of values covered by the shaded bar. The range of values is between 100 and 325. Next, check each answer choice. Which equation results in a value between 100 and 325? Answer choice **A**, 500 ÷ 4 = 125. This is the correct answer. The other answer choices are **B:** 500 ÷ 100 = 5; **C:** 500 × 4 = 2,000; and **D:** 500 × 100 = 50,000. None of these values falls within the shaded portion of the number line.

12. **H** 24 × 58 = 1,392. If you had difficulty finding this answer, you may need to practice multiplication. Complete Mile 5 to review multiplication. If you simply made a careless mistake, slow down when you take the test.

13. **C** Because $\frac{4}{9}$ is less than $\frac{7}{9}$, you don't have to borrow to solve this subtraction problem. Even better, because the two fractions have the same denominator, all you have to do is subtract the numerators. $\frac{7}{9} - \frac{4}{9} = \frac{3}{9}$; 5 – 4 = 1. Therefore, $5\frac{7}{9} - 4\frac{4}{9} = 1\frac{3}{9}$, which reduces to $1\frac{1}{3}$.

14. **H** It usually is best to rewrite this type of problem so that the numbers are stacked one on top of another. Rewrite the numbers so that they have an equal number of digits to the right of the decimal place. Write the problem this way.

$$\begin{array}{r} 0.5 \\ 2.2 \\ \underline{+\ 29.0} \end{array}$$

Now add as you would with whole numbers, remembering to place a decimal point below the column of decimal points in your addition problem. The answer is 31.7.

15. **C** To compare numbers with decimals, you must compare numbers in the same decimal places in each number, moving from left to right from the decimal point. Compare the tenths places first, then the hundredths, then the thousandths, and so on. You only have to compare until you find a pair of digits that are not equal. If the tenths digits are not equal, for example, you do not need to compare the hundredths or thousandths digits. Simply compare the tenths digits and you are done: The number with the larger number in the tenths digit has the greater value. If a decimal stops before you have finished comparing, simply add zeros to the end of the number until it has the same number of decimal places as the other numbers. In this question you only need to compare values to the tenths place. 8 is greater than 7, so 3.802 is greater than 3.7254.

16. **J** There are three girls in the group of seven club members. Therefore, if one club member is chosen at random to represent the club, the chances that the club member will be a girl are three in seven, or $\frac{3}{7}$. To calculate probability, you must compare the part (girls) to the whole (members of the club), not one part to another. That is why the answer $\frac{3}{4}$ is incorrect—it compares the number of girls to the number of boys, not the number of girls to all the members of the club.

17. **C** An obtuse angle is one that measures between 90° and 180°. A right corner measures exactly 90° (answer choice **A**). An acute angle is one that measures less than 90° (answer choice **B**). There is no special name for an angle that measures less than 45°. If you need more practice with these definitions, review Mile 24.

18. **H** This pattern repeats every three shapes. The 1st shape is the same as the 4th, the 2nd is the same as the 5th, and the 3rd is the same as the 6th. The 7th shape will be the same as the 1st, the 8th shape will be the same as the 2nd, and the 9th shape will be the same as the 3rd.

19. **D** The mode is the number that appears most often in a group of numbers. The number 13 appears twice in the table, while all of the other numbers appear only once. Therefore, 13 is the mode of this data set. Review Mile 36 if you feel you need more practice finding the mode of a data set.

20. **G** A mile is approximately 1.5 kilometers. Therefore, 2 miles is approximately 3 kilometers. You can review the approximate comparisons of metric and U.S. customary lengths by completing Mile 28.

21. **D** The area of a rectangle is calculated by multiplying the lengths of its sides. Multiply each pair of numbers in the answer choices. The correct pair will result in a product of 24. That answer is 8 cm by 3 cm: $8 \times 3 = 24$.

22. **H** Each of the circles in the correct answer has the same fraction shaded.

    In answer choice **F**, the first circle is $\frac{1}{2}$ shaded and the second is $\frac{1}{4}$ shaded.
    In answer choice **G**, the first circle is $\frac{1}{3}$ shaded and the second is $\frac{1}{4}$ shaded.
    In answer choice **H**, the first circle is $\frac{1}{3}$ shaded and the second is $\frac{2}{6}$ shaded.
    $\frac{2}{6}$ is equal to $\frac{1}{3}$. Answer choice **H** is correct. In answer choice **J**, the first circle is $\frac{2}{4}$ shaded and the second is $\frac{4}{6}$ shaded. Review Mile 18 if you need more practice comparing fractions.

23. **B** One way to find the correct answer to this problem is to test each answer choice until you find the correct one. Does $5 \times 5 = 30$? No, $5 \times 5 = 25$. Therefore, answer choice **A** cannot be correct. How about 5×6? That does equal 30, so choice **B** is the correct answer! The variable is equal to 6.

24. **G** Because each fraction in the answer choices has a numerator of 1, you only have to compare the denominators of these fractions. Remember that a smaller denominator means the whole is divided into fewer parts. Therefore, $\frac{1}{2}$ is greater than $\frac{1}{3}$, $\frac{1}{6}$, or $\frac{1}{10}$. The correct answer is $\frac{1}{2}$.

25. **A** A point on the coordinate grid is named by two numbers. The first number tells you how far to the right of zero the point is located. The second number tells you how far up from zero the point is located. The point on this coordinate grid is located three units to the right and five units up. Therefore, its location is (3, 5). You can review coordinate points by completing Mile 26.

26. **J** You can use POE to get rid of the incorrect answer choices in this question. The correct answer must show a stem-and-leaf plot that lists 18 values. Only the correct answer lists 18 values; answer choices **F** and **G** list fewer values, and answer choice **H** lists 19 values. If you need to review stem-and-leaf plots, complete Mile 35.

27. **A** This pattern is formed by adding 9 to the previous number: 45 = 36 + 9, 54 = 45 + 9, and so on. The numbers that will follow 63 in the pattern are 72 and 81.

28. **G** To answer this question, you must remember that the ten-thousandths place in a decimal is four places to the right of the decimal point. Because you are looking for a decimal that equals "seven and one hundred-six ten-thousandths," you must find an answer choice that extends exactly four places to the right of the decimal point. Only answer choice **G** does this. Therefore, you can use POE to get rid of answer choices **F**, **H**, and **J**.

29. **C** Eliminate answer choice **A**, which is a unit used to measure length, because you are looking for a unit that measures weight. A cruise ship is a very heavy item, so you would want to use a large unit to measure its weight. That is why choice **C** is the best answer.

30. **H** Here is an easy way to solve this type of problem. Count the number of minutes that have gone by from the starting time until the end of the hour. Then count the number of complete hours between the hour and the ending time. Finally, count the number of minutes that have gone by from the beginning of the hour until the ending time.

In this problem there are 15 minutes from the starting time of 10:45 A.M. to the end of the hour. There are 2 complete hours: 11 A.M. to 12 P.M., and 12 P.M. to 1 P.M.. There are 16 minutes from the beginning of the hour of 1 P.M. to the ending time of 1:16 P.M. Janet's hike was 2 hours and 15 + 16 = 31 minutes long.

31. **A** You can compare fractions by using the cross-multiplication method. Multiply the denominator of each fraction by the numerator of the other. Write the products by the numerators. The fraction with the larger number next to its numerator is the larger fraction. Only choice A, $\frac{3}{12}$, is smaller than $\frac{2}{7}$. Review the bowtie method by completing Mile 16.

32. **H** To find the mean of a set of numbers, add the numbers together. Then divide by however many numbers are in the set. In this problem there are four numbers in the set. The sum of the four numbers is 35 + 42 + 29 + 46 = 152. Divide 152 by 4 to find the correct answer, which is 38. Don't forget that you are allowed to use your calculator on this part of the test! Review Mile 36 if you feel you need more practice finding averages.

33. **C** Alison teaches four classes. Each class has eight students in it. How many students does she have? 8 + 8 + 8 + 8 = 32. Remember that 8 + 8 + 8 + 8 is the same as 8×4. Therefore, you can find S, the total number of students Alison teaches, with the open sentence $8 \times 4 = S$.

34. **H** Find the mean of the set of numbers by adding the numbers together. Then divide by however many numbers are in the set. There are four prices in this set of data. The sum of the four numbers is 28 + 34 + 30 + 32 = 124. Divide 124 by 4 to get $31, which is the correct answer. You are allowed to use your calculator on this part of the test, so be sure to use it!

35. **B** This question isn't easy. If you got it right, pat yourself on the back! The pattern is actually made up of two different patterns. One pattern is formed by the 1st, 3rd, and 5th numbers—each is two less than the one before it (20, 18, 16, 14, ...). The other pattern is formed by the 2nd, 4th, and 6th numbers in the pattern. Each number in that pattern is also two less than the number before it (26, 24, 22, ...). The next number in the pattern will be two less than 22. Therefore, 20 is the correct answer.

36. **J** This triangle has equal sides that are 2 inches in length. The perimeter of a triangle is the sum of the lengths of its sides, so the perimeter of this triangle is 2 + 2 + 2 = 6 inches.

37. **B** Two out of eight triangles in the original figure are shaded. Therefore, $\frac{1}{4}$ of the figure is shaded. The figure shown in answer choice **B** is also $\frac{1}{4}$ shaded, so choice **F** is the correct answer. Review Miles 15, 16, and 18 if you want more practice with this type of question.

38. **J** To answer this question, you must remember that the hundredths place in a decimal is two places to the right of the decimal point. Review each answer choice until you find one with a 7 two places to the right of the decimal point. Answer choice **J**, 428.573, is the only one. If you chose answer choice **F**, 761.035, you chose the answer with a 7 in the hundreds place. If you are having trouble telling the *hundreds* place and *hundredths* place apart, reread Mile 9.

39. **D** The open sentence $200 \times Y = 600$ asks you to find a number that you can multiply by 200 to get 600. Which answer choice poses the same question? Answer choice **A** tells you to multiply 200 and 600, so this is not the correct answer. Answer choice **B** tells you to subtract 200 from 600. Answer choice **C** tells you to divide. Therefore, the answer must be choice **D.** It asks how much money each student contributed to the charity: *Y*, the amount each student contributed, times 200, the number of students, will equal 600, the number of dollars contributed by all the students combined.

40. **H** You can use POE to help you solve this question. Choose one piece of data from the table, such as Brenda's twelve goals. Now check each bar graph and eliminate the ones in which Brenda is shown to have scored something other than twelve goals. Answer choices **F** and **J** show that Brenda scored ten goals, so they can be eliminated. Repeat this process with another piece of data to help you eliminate choice **G.**

41. **C** Put your finger on June 2 at the bottom of the graph and then run your finger straight up until you touch the line showing the attendance at the game. Keeping your finger on the line, look at the numbers running up the left margin of the graph. Where is your finger in relation to the numbers? Your finger should be between 5,000 and 6,000. That means the attendance at the June 2nd game was between those two numbers. Only answer choice **C**, 5,200, is between 5,000 and 6,000, so it has to be the correct answer.

42. **G** Perimeter tells you the distance around something. You would need to know the distance around a garden in order to surround it with fencing. To paint a wall (answer choice **F**), you would need to know the area of the wall. To calculate the time it would take to take a trip (answer choice **H**), you would need to calculate speed. To determine how much milk a bucket holds (answer choice **J**), you would need to know volume.

43. **A** An obtuse triangle is a triangle with one obtuse angle. An obtuse angle is one that measures between 90° and 180°. Only the triangle shown in answer choice **A** is obtuse.

44. **J** To round a decimal to the nearest hundredth, look at the digit in the thousandths place. If the digit is less than 5, eliminate that digit and every digit to its right. If the digit is 5 or more, add 1 to the digit in the tenths place and then eliminate the thousandths digit and every other digit to its right. Because the thousandths digit in 1.476 is 6, you should add 1 to the hundredths digit. The result is 1.48.

45. **C** The average human body temperature is about 37°C. You can review this and other important Celsius values in Mile 31.

46. **G** The best way to answer this problem is by using POE. Answer choice **F** presents a question that can be answered using division. Answer choices **H** and **J** present questions that can be answered using addition. Therefore, you can eliminate every answer choice except the correct one.

    Because probability is used to calculate the likelihood that something will happen, it would be useful to figure out how likely Minerva is to select an 8 randomly from the pile of cards. Review Mile 42 if you want to work on more probability problems.

47. **C** To find the answer to this question, you must calculate the area and perimeter of each rectangle in the answer choices. Answer choice **A** has sides of 3 and 4, so its area is $3 \times 4 = 12$ and its perimeter is $3 + 4 + 3 + 4 = 14$. Its area does not equal its perimeter, so choice **A** is not the correct answer. Repeat the process for each answer choice until you find the correct answer. Answer choice **B** has sides of 1 and 5, so its area is 5 and its perimeter is 12. Answer choice **C** has sides of 3 and 6, so its area and perimeter both equal 18. Answer choice **D** has sides of 4 and 5, so its area is 20 and its perimeter is 18.

48. **G** Because $D = 8$, substitute 8 for D in the problem. You should get $48 \div 8 = 6$. If you were not sure how to find the correct answer to this question, review Miles 6 and 45.

49. **B** To answer this question, you must determine the value of each tick mark on the number line. This number line is divided into units of 3. Write 15, 18, 21, 24, and 27 under the tick marks between 12 and 30. Point *K*, which is four tick marks to the right of 30, has a value of 42. Fill in the values under the tick marks to the right of 30 to make sure that you are right.

50. **G** This pattern is formed by adding a new number to each addition problem. The new number is always one greater than the number that was previously added. $1 + 2 + 3 + 4 + 5 = 15$ is the fourth sum in the sequence. Therefore, $1 + 2 + 3 + 4 + 5 + 6 = 21$ is the fifth sum in the sequence. $1 + 2 + 3 + 4 + 5 + 6 + 7 = 28$ is the sixth sum in the sequence.

51. **A** Suzy has five more comic books than Jim has. Jim has *y* comic books, so Suzie has $y + 5$ comic books.

    Another way to answer this problem is to replace *y* with a number. Say that Jim has ten comic books. Suzy has five more than Jim, so she has fifteen comic books. Which answer choice equals fifteen when $y = 10$? Only answer choice **A**, so it must be the correct answer.

52. **J** First, count the number of minutes that go by from the starting time until the end of the hour. Then, count the number of complete hours between the hour and the ending time. Finally, count the number of minutes that go by from the beginning of the hour until the ending time.

    In this problem there are 15 minutes from the starting time of 7:45 A.M. to the end of the hour. There are 6 complete hours between 8 P.M. and 2 P.M. There are 25 minutes from the beginning of the hour, 2 P.M., to the ending time of 1:25 P.M. Manuela's school day is 6 hours + 15 minutes + 25 minutes = 6 hours and 40 minutes long.

53. **A** The decimal model is divided into boxes of one hundred equal squares. Therefore, the decimal model represents a decimal that extends to the hundredths place. One box is completely shaded, so it represents the whole value 1. The other has 28 shaded squares, representing the decimal value 0.28. Together, the boxes represent the value 1.28.

54. **J** Parallel lines are lines that never meet, like the lines shown in the illustration. A ray (answer choice **F**) has one endpoint and extends without end away from that endpoint. Perimeter (answer choice **G**) is the measure of the distance around a polygon. You calculate perimeter by adding the lengths of all the sides of a polygon. Perpendicular lines (answer choice **H**) are lines that meet at right corners.

55. **C** Answer this problem by creating a sample space. Use one letter to represent each type of pet: D for dog, P for parrot, C for cat, and S for snake. Make a sample space listing all the different possible combinations of two different pets.

DP	CD
DC	CP
DS	CS
PD	SD
PC	SP
PS	SC

Next, eliminate doubles. DS and SD are doubles because in both cases, Linda buys a snake and a dog. Here is what the list looks like after all doubles are eliminated.

DP	PC
DC	PS
DS	CS

Now find the answer choice that matches this list exactly.

56. **G** A quart and a liter are about the same amount of liquid. Therefore, 2 quarts of juice is approximately 2 liters of juice. You can review approximate comparisons of metric liquid measures and U.S. customary liquid measures by completing Mile 30.

57. **A** There are six numbers on the number cube. Three of the numbers—2, 4, and 6—are even. Therefore, Aretha has a three in six, or $\frac{3}{6}$, chance of rolling an even number. $\frac{3}{6}$ reduces to $\frac{1}{2}$, which is the correct answer. Review Mile 42 if you want to work on more probability problems.

58. **H** This pattern is created by subtracting 7 from the previous value in the pattern. $42 - 7 = 35$; $35 - 7 = 28$. The number missing from the pattern is $28 - 7 = 21$. Complete Mile 39 to get more practice working with number patterns.

59. **D** To compare seven-digit numbers, compare corresponding digits from left to right. Start with the millions digit. If they are not equal, your work is done. Whichever number has the larger millions digit is the larger number. If the digits are equal, compare the hundred-thousands digit, then the ten-thousands digit, then the thousands digit, and so on until you find a pair of digits that are not equal.

    To compare the numbers in the correct answer, you must compare the ten-thousands digits. 7 is greater than 6, so 8,871,302 is greater than 8,864,924.

60. **J** This pattern is the alphabet with a special twist: Every 3rd letter is capitalized. The 12th letter in this pattern will be capitalized, then, because the 3rd, 6th, and 9th letters are capitalized. What is the 12th letter of the alphabet? It is L, so the answer is "capital L."